To Phil,
Keep cooling it's, too late!

Simon Wyatt

Darling Phil
Happy Christmas
love Ingrid xx
2005

Simon Wright

The Wright Taste
Recipes and other stories

" *The most wanted food critic in Britain today* **"**
Gordon Ramsay

" *I can't see it – I think even getting a bit of mud on him and he's going to be a bit Oooh, I don't like this stuff!* **"**
Heston Blumenthal

Published in 2008 by Gomer Press, Llandysul, Ceredigion, SA44 4JL

ISBN 978 1 84323 917 8

A CIP record for this title is available from the British Library.

© Copyright text: Simon Wright, 2008

© Copyright photographs unless otherwise noted: Julian Castaldi, 2008

This book accompanies the television series *The Wright Taste*, an Indus Films/Vox production for BBC Wales.

Simon Wright asserts his moral right under the Copyright, Designs and Patents Act, 1988
to be identified respectively as author of this work.

This book is published with the financial support of the Welsh Books Council.

Printed and bound in Wales at Gomer Press, Llandysul, Ceredigion

Simon Wright

The Wright Taste
Recipes and other stories

Photographs by Julian Castaldi

Farmer? He looks more like a food critic to me.
Shaun Hill

Contents

Foreword

“ I've known the name Simon Wright for a long time but have only known the man well for about three years. I actually appeared on the cover of his last book, *Tough Cookies*, but was unaware of it until publication! This time I have been asked to write the foreword and I'm honoured to do so.

I have always been aware of Simon's great passion and equally great values and principles when it comes to food and cooking. This book is testament to how deep the roots and foundations of his passion, values and principles lie.

Simon is no chef but he is as knowledgeable as most. He understands perfectly that you can't make a silk purse from a sow's ear! That the greater the quality and better sourced your ingredient is, then the better the end result will be. Yes, you may have to look a bit further or pay a little more but as Simon clearly demonstrates, it is worth it.

What impresses me most is how far one man is prepared to go to show us the difference. I hope, like me, you will be left inspired. ”

Stephen Terry
*Chef proprietor, The Hardwick, Abergavenny
and winner of The Great British Menu 2008*

Introduction

It's a rainy day in April. I'm sliding down a steep slope on my rear end, trammelling up grass and mud with my boots, sending twigs and stones shooting into the field below my descent. This isn't a controlled slide and I'm trying to bring it to a rapid end by clutching on to passing branches but they are either slippery wet or rotten and it takes the base of a hefty oak to finally terminate my fall. Along the way I've picked up a few grazes and my upper arm is sore from the impact with the tree. There's nothing broken though, and given that I'm alone in this little crevice in the countryside, I've not suffered any embarrassment either. I am being watched, though. Looking up 30 feet or so, towards the top of the bank that I just descended at such an impressive pace, two ewes are peering at me with expressions of bewilderment. It would be easy to imagine that it was the frenzied sight of my tumble that set these bemused looks on their faces but that would be fanciful – they always look like that. The reason that they're staring at me at all is simply to make sure that they remain at a distance where there is no prospect of me being able to grab hold of them. They have every reason to be confident; I've been chasing them now for the best part of 90 minutes in the vain hope that I can somehow persuade them to return to the field where they belong – a massive field in which they can dwell in some luxury with only another 10 of their companions. Two of which are their children. The lambs are making it very clear they want their mothers back. The ewes are clearly just as distressed about the situation. Me, I'm just trying to bring everyone back together. I'm an angel of mercy but operating in conditions of deep suspicion. None of these animals has a gram of trust in my motives and they will do all they can to thwart me.

It's raining harder now and I notice my car keys have gone from my pocket. They've fallen out at some point during the drop and must be lodged on the bank somewhere. I start to scramble back up the slope, studying the vegetation like a botanist – which is the signal for the sheep to scuttle by in the opposite direction into the open field below. It's not dark yet, but it's getting there.

How did I get here? I love the countryside and I'm wedded to the beauty of rural west Wales – I took my vows on that one many years ago and I can tell you without risk of exposure that I've been faithful ever since – but I'm a stranger to the soil; I have writer's hands, soft and uncalloused for a man in his forties. My relationship with the land has never been a physical one. As for animals, I've admired them from afar; it's never been a touchy-feely thing. Yet here I find myself scrambling up a grassy bank in pursuit of a couple of sheep.

It ended up in a field but it began in bed. I woke up thinking about the restaurant that I own with my wife Maryann and our partners Sue and Mark. It's a restaurant built on ingredients. That's not literally true, of course – it's actually built on land that's a mixture of mud and shale, I imagine, though, unusually, a powerful stream runs underneath it too. But the restaurant *offering* is founded on the produce that we buy. It's a simple philosophy – perhaps we're simple people – but we share the view that great cooking demands the use of great ingredients. The job of the chef and the restaurant is to do just enough work to bring out the real splendour of those raw materials. That last bit's not easy, because it requires taste, understanding and skill. And then there's another problem: you have to find those great ingredients in the first place.

At a restaurant like ours, a lot of work goes into that last bit. Again, it's not as easy as it might seem. You have to find the produce, seek it out; sometimes it comes looking for you but often it doesn't. Then you have to work with producers, get a dialogue going, make sure that they really understand what you're after. And finally you have to afford it and work out how you can incorporate all this great stuff into your menu and remain an affordable and reasonably-priced place to eat. So I woke up thinking about salad leaf and one or two vegetables that it's not easy to get hold of and I remembered my father-in-law's land, thirty acres of it, mostly lying fallow. The early morning sun was streaming in through the rooflight and I could picture the view from the land on a golden autumn day like this, crystal clear across the Tywi valley and on to the Black Mountains and the Brecons. I saw freshly tilled soil, crumbly and red-brown with virgin green shoots and tips just visible and sprinkled with dew. And then I glimpsed myself, healthy and tanned, pulling up a few carrots and gathering them in a wicker basket ready for the restaurant kitchen.

This was about 7.00am. By 9.00 I'd recalled my previous attempts at gardening, short-lived with results characterised by neglect. I wouldn't have the patience, the attention to detail. By 9.30 I had realised that pigs were the thing: why couldn't we produce some of our own pork? How exciting would it be to bring our own meat to the restaurant table? And why stop at pork? Why not lamb and chicken? Why not beef even?

I described my vision to Maryann over a cup of coffee. This may have been one of those occasions where somewhere, in the recesses of my mind, I was secretly relying on a veto. That would have allowed me to contemplate the

whole enterprise in the safe knowledge that it would never happen, content that if I hadn't been obstructed then it would surely have been a perfect success. If my subconscious was depending on this as a strategy to avoid disaster, it was to be disappointed. Maryann has always been keen on animals and she liked the idea. By lunchtime we'd told a whole load of other people. I'd locked myself in and thrown the key into the river. This was going to happen; I was going to do some farming.

There was another thing, too, by way of motivation. For much of the past decade I'd sat on my ever-expanding rear-end criticising other people's efforts to serve me good food. I understood how hard the best chefs worked; after all, I ran my own restaurants. But I'd never really delved much further back than that in the chain of food production. I was the first one to say it was all about the ingredients but I didn't really know very much about what went into making those ingredients good. Well, here was a chance to find out, to take on the challenge of producing meat good enough for the table of a really good restaurant. I was up for it, even if it did mean getting my hands dirty.

The chapters that follow are intended to give a flavour of my foray into farming and each one is followed by a little interjection from my friend Mark Manson, a partner in our restaurant and a familiar face to anyone who watched the series on TV. The book also contains a stash of recipes and I would like to pretend that I created them but they are mostly based on information provided by my wife Maryann and merely interpreted by me. Most emanate from dishes cooked at our restaurant, Y Polyn, so the credit should also go to partner and chef Sue Manson and the other two mainstays of our kitchen team, Alix Alliston and Catrin Thomas.

Lamb

As I wound my way up into the hinterland of the Cothi valley I carried with me a mental picture of Wyn Jones, farmer of sheep. We had spoken on the phone a couple of times and the tone of his voice seemed to keep time with the landscape – as unhurried and relaxed as the easy curves of the hills, but solid as stone too, rock-heavy with experience. In my mind I saw an old man, white-haired, weathered by the seasons, wiry but fiercely strong, stern and taciturn. As it turned out, I was way off the mark – he was a young bull of a guy a few years my junior, seated on a quad bike in his farmyard, a Llanelli Scarlets cap perched on his boulder of a head, grinning like a baby. It wasn't that I'd heard wrong – there was age in his accent – but the tenor of his voice was drawn from deep roots, drilled down through generations, buried in the hills.

That I was wrong came as something of a relief. As it was, this whole episode had made me feel like an embarrassed child. I knew nothing of this world and my naivety made me squirm. Even making the phone call in the first place had been a struggle; I didn't know if I'd even be understood – a stranger calling up out of the blue in pursuit of a handful of rare-breed sheep, having no previous association with animal husbandry, asking the dumbest of questions. There was a sketch once in *Not The Nine O'clock News* where a guy enters a specialist hi-fi store and asks to buy a 'gramophone'. Two assistants take turns to ridicule his innocence, asking him if he wants various components which he doesn't recognise. In his eagerness not to seem an idiot the customer quickly consents to everything they suggest: 'woofers, tweeters etc' and eventually, 'a bag on your head' with which they happily furnish him. I could feel the polythene resting gently on my ears.

I think Wyn did find it all faintly amusing but he wasn't about to show it. He had that graciousness that came from knowing he was on his own territory and holding all the cards – but not wanting you to feel that way. I'd arrived at his farm, just ten or so miles from my home, by a circuitous route. Sheep, or more accurately lamb, had been my first thought when I embarked on this little journey into smallholding and I'd made some vague enquiries of farming acquaintances. Securing the animals didn't appear to be anything of a problem; there's no shortage of sheep in west Wales and I could either go to a market or sort out a deal privately. Something was missing, though. I knew when it came to pigs or cattle or poultry that choosing the breed was going to be at the centre of things in my efforts to produce the best quality meat. With sheep, it was less certain. A few people recommended different breeds but I didn't get any sense of the advocacy, the passion that you find in someone who champions the flavour of, for instance, Gloucester Old Spot pork as triumphant over all others. Mostly, when I asked about equating breed to flavour I just didn't get anywhere, but what I did hear plenty about was size and how quickly it could be acquired.

I can't pretend I wasn't disappointed. For someone who has made a rickety career out of quality food, much of it in Wales, it could only be unsettling to hear so little about the thing that concerned me most – how these animals would taste when they finally ended up on the plate. But it's not difficult to understand the preoccupation with growth and financial returns. The economics of farming were a mystery when I set out and now, a little way down the line, the fog has only slightly cleared, but even I can see it's a marginal existence. To get anything like a decent return you need your ewes to be bearing lambs that will fetch the best price at market, and that price is mostly dependent on weight. It's a simple equation but one that's hard to argue with. For me, though, since I was just dabbling in something that is a livelihood to others, there was the luxury of choosing another priority: flavour. And I was determined to dig deeper.

The first clue fell at my feet, literally. *The Guardian* newspaper was going through one of its promotional tics, publishing wallcharts on various subjects and inserting them into their broadsheet. I took little notice, my habit being to start with the sport, flick through the news and maybe read the odd feature. The thing about newspapers these days is that other stuff tumbles out of them, sometimes before you even leave the newsagent's. This one hit the floor as I made coffee in my kitchen and lay there half-open, a couple of pictures peeking out – drawings of animals. Sheep to be precise.

The poster was dedicated to British breeds and the very first entry was a dark brown, fluffy specimen called a Balwen. A phrase jumped out at me immediately: 'native to the Towy valley.' My valley. The name of the breed meant nothing to me but it seemed that I'd been given a little sign. Checking on the web, I discovered it was true enough, and what's more I found an enchanting little story – Balwens had been unique to the Tywi valley but had been all but wiped out in the fierce flooding of 1947. Just one ram had remained, so all the present Balwens were derived from that ram. I was smitten.

'The flavour is the thing about them. If you put two plates of lamb in front of me on the table, I could tell you which was the Balwen every time.'

I'd just asked Wyn about the taste and, for just about the first time, I'd got the kind of answer I was looking for. Not, 'Well, one lamb tastes much like another,' or 'Yes, they taste very nice, you get a lot of meat on the bone', but a genuine opinion that this breed tasted better than others. I put the phone down, elated by this good news. I'd found Wyn's details on the internet site for the Balwen sheep society, which showed that there were small flocks all over the UK but Wyn Jones was by far the closest to me, just a few miles north.

Those that know the Tywi valley will mostly recall its snaking run past the market towns of Llandovery, Llandeilo and Carmarthen. It has a gentle beauty that catches you unawares. The charm is subtle and it's a slow seduction; this isn't a landscape that flutters its eyelashes, flashes a little stocking and calls for more champagne. This is a landscape you hold hands with at sunset or sunrise; it might be a while before you even realise you've fallen for her, but once you're hooked, she's got you for good. She got me twenty years ago and I've never been tempted to stray. There's more to it than the river valley, though; skip off into the backroads, leaving the A40 far behind, and there's a tangle of slender lanes weaving their way through tiny hamlets, past whitewashed farms, lonely chapels, the ruins of abandoned mills. You can easily get lost here and I still do, sometimes wilfully.

I found Waunfawr farm, though, along with Wyn and his bike. Wyn told me to climb on the back and I did so, facing rearwards as we buzzed through the lanes to where the Balwens roamed. We had the film crew in pursuit and

Wyn's mother told me quietly that the night before, her son had been nervous about the filming. The thing is, I too had started this whole escapade feeling nervous about the filming, but our director Pip made the whole thing so easy just by staying out of the way and letting it flow. As we spun back and forth around the field trying to get a better look at the sheep I questioned Wyn about the breed and he answered easily, effortlessly, as relaxed as if the cameras weren't there.

Not much later I discovered that more effort had gone into Wyn's performance than I thought. When I'd mentioned the whole Balwen story on the phone to him, he'd seemed ignorant of the tale of flooding and the one remaining ram. 'Good God! is that true?" he'd said in response. Consequently it had occurred to me I might tell the story to him again, on camera, with the sheep all around us. It didn't work out that way. Wyn had clearly been in secret rehearsals and when I asked him to tell me a bit about Balwens it was if he'd been waiting for the starting pistol.

'Well, the thing is, Simon, back when there was all that flooding in 1947 . . .'

Wyn was great on camera, but it was nothing more than a reflection of his generous nature. We did a deal for some ewes 'with lambs at foot' which basically meant that the difficult part, lambing, had been taken care of for this year. We took the lot of them back to the land where they were to share about 7 acres with just a couple of Welsh Black cattle who were yet to move in. This bit of pasture hadn't seen a farm animal for the best part of twenty years, and nothing chemical had gone near the ground for at least that long. My father-in-law had planted hundreds of trees there over the years, so there was natural shade and the grass was meadow-like, thick with wild flowers and herbs. As long as the lambs were thriving then I didn't plan to give them anything in the way of extra feed or supplements; it was my guess that there were riches enough growing all around them.

The sheep were my first experience of keeping farm animals. When I look

back on it now it doesn't seem such a big deal – just a few lambs and their mothers. It soon became clear that they didn't take too much looking after, just a little attention to their feet and, of course, shearing in early summer. In other words, a manicure and a radical change of hairstyle, a beauty treatment for ovines. But at the outset I was nervous. My knowledge was scant and what I did know I'd only picked up from books, nothing practical. Somehow I didn't feel worthy of the responsibility and had a feeling that there was trouble ahead.

*

After a couple of days I was thinking my fears were misplaced. I was really taking to farming. At the desk, working on the laptop, I'd be itching to get outside again, thinking, I'll give it another half an hour and then I'll go and check on the animals. Maybe I'll take a sandwich with me, sit in the sun for a while, take in the view across the valley. There was even the possibility that I might fall asleep on the grass – I was beginning to appreciate the strictures of this new world of animal husbandry. It meant I had no choice but to go outside, walk the fields, gorge on the fresh air. It wasn't an indulgence, not one of those instances where I feel I really should be doing something else; it was an obligation, a responsibility. In a way it was what I *hoped* might happen – it was *good* for me, life was *better* with the animals.

When I reached the land, there was no sign of any livestock. Already I knew this to be not unusual – sometimes the sheep were right up against the gate but more usually they were in some distant corner of the field, out of sight, covered by vegetation or the lie of the land. I squinted into the distance, looking for dark shapes amongst the tall grass and through the fresh foliage of the trees and bushes. Nothing. So I traipsed further into the field and over the little rise towards the far edge of the land where the boundary is swallowed-up

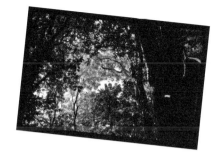

by a greedy tangle of brambles. Still no sign of any of the creatures. It was the hardest job I'd had finding them but I registered only a small flicker of concern; I'd already discovered that a dozen sheep can find easy camouflage in this kind of mixed terrain.

And then I heard a rustling up ahead, just at the point where the advancing tide of briars gives way to the lush grass. I stopped and stared. Motionless, not ten yards away, a full grown, sleek and seemingly relaxed red fox returned my gaze. For a second or two our eyes locked. There was no panic on the animal's part, just an apparent acceptance that it was time to leave, so he turned tail and trotted off calmly into the undergrowth. I'd seen a fox around here before and taken pleasure in spotting it. Not now. I checked the immediate area with a fear of what I might find. The truth was I didn't know whether I should be concerned or not. Random flashes of fox-related information darted around my head, little snippets that I must have picked up over the years – foxes don't often attack lambs in daylight, the presence of the ewes deters them, isn't it only the newly-born and sickly that are really vulnerable? The trouble was I didn't know if these recollections had any truth in them or not and I couldn't attach any weight to them. So I continued to scour the bushes and check the hedges, grateful that there was no sign of the mauled and bloody carcass that kept appearing as an image in my head.

But I still needed to find the sheep, so I hurried down the slope to the eastern boundary to view the only part of the field I hadn't yet covered. Before long I caught sight of them, about a hundred yards away, bunched together as always, the lambs spring-loaded, rolling and tumbling, the ewes suspicious and quick to scarper as soon I got too close for their liking. But there was something unusual this time. One of the ewes lagged a little behind the others and every few yards turned to face me, letting out a sharp, tremulous bleat. There was something in the shaky vibrato of the tone, something that smacked of panic and shrill desperation. I tried to count the lambs; it's not

easy because they don't keep still and they all look the same. Five – that can't be right, there should seven. Count again: six; count again: six; count once more to be certain: still six. One was definitely missing. As the ewe turned again to face me it became obvious what was up. Her cries were directed at me; she'd lost her lamb and she was asking me to do something about it. She was pleading.

I shuddered. Only two days into this journey and it looked like I was a lamb down already. A darkness began to descend and anxiety had worked its way into my stomach. What if I lost another tonight? The fox would have a taste for it now, surely, and I'd heard tales of repeated raids, night after night, a lamb or two at a time until the fox is tracked down and killed. A Peter Paul and Mary song we used to sing in infant school, seeps into my skull, the trickle of melody soon becoming a torrent . . .

The fox went out on a chilly night,
He prayed for the moon to give him light,
For he'd many a mile to go that night,
Before he reached the town-o, town-o, town-o,
He'd many a mile to go that night,
Before he reached the town-o.

He ran till he came to a great big pen,
Where the ducks and the geese were put therein,
"A couple of you will grease my chin,
Before I leave this town-o, town-o, town-o,
A couple of you will grease my chin,
Before I leave this town-o."

He grabbed the gray goose by the neck,
Throwed a duck across his back,
He didn't mind their quack, quack, quack,
And their legs a-dangling down-o, down-o, down-o,
He didn't mind their quack, quack, quack,
And their legs a-dangling down-o.

I could picture the cartoon fox from the songbook, his greedy grin, his greasy chin, but at least there was no mention of lambs. I thought about camping out that night, lighting a fire, but dismissed it as a ridiculous notion. I don't even have a tent and how many nights could I keep that up? But then shepherds do it, don't they? Night after night on a hillside, holed up in a stone hut, a campfire burning through until dawn; I wondered if they still did that anywhere?   Maybe on a Greek island somewhere.   All I knew was that somehow the fox had to be stopped. I thought about calling someone, someone with a shotgun, someone who could flush it out. Get it killed.

I heard the squeal of tyres as I made this ethical handbrake turn, I smelt the burning rubber and the bitter aroma of principles going up in smoke. I was always, vaguely, on the side of the fox. Not as a matter of great principle but just because it kind of went with all the other stuff I believe in. And then without warning I'm standing on the border looking over to the other side. The side with the flat caps, the wax jackets, the Land Rovers and the twelve-bores. If I had a gun now, and a clear shot at the fox, I honestly believe I'd pull the trigger. Weird. I break into a cold sweat at the implications. After six months of this, could I really be marching with the Countryside Alliance?

I ran back to where I'd seen the fox, certain now that there was a corpse to be found. But as I passed close to the boundary fence I heard a cry from the neighbouring field, and there was the lamb, distressed but unharmed, calling out for its mother. I guessed that the fox must have heard it too and sensed an

opportunity. Whether the predator would have capitalised, I don't know, but a couple of days later I was up at dawn and saw it again, this time from a hundred yards or more away. It was trotting through the remains of the morning mist, bisecting the loose gathering of sheep and lambs as it went on its way. For their part, they took little notice, continuing to chew on the grass. One or two looked up but showed no alarm and little interest, as if the fox passed that way every day around that time. I rested on the gate and thought about what I had seen in relation to the panic of a few days before, but I couldn't make any sense of it.

*

Much as I'd like to pretend that raising these lambs was an epic struggle, the truth is, it was pretty undemanding. Like Wyn said, Balwens will 'live on a stone' and with acre after acre of lush grass available to them they weren't being asked to do anything remotely of the sort. Not that they were grateful. With the other animals there was always, in one form or another, some sense of an understanding that I was there to provide for them in some way. The other livestock associated me with food and water and, as a consequence, they gave the impression that they were pleased to see me. I was happy to play along with the idea that there was some genuine fondness on their part because it made me feel wanted, and anyway, whilst ultimately the relationship was about food production and what I had planned for them couldn't really be called the actions of a true friend, I did develop a real affection for them. I felt a warmth towards the sheep, too, but it was unrequited. When they arrived, there wasn't an ounce of trust, and months later, they were down to total cynicism. They hated the sight of me. I couldn't get within 20 yards before they'd bolt off across the field, making it clear that I was right at the bottom of their popularity list, below the fox that they'd let walk right by them.

I wasn't losing sleep over it, though. I could handle the contempt of a bunch of woolly animals. The problem was, it made looking after them so much harder. For a start, they'd escape. I'd been warned about this by more than one farming friend when I told them I was buying Balwens. Apparently they were specialists at it, and few fences could hold them. So when they got out, which in the early stages they did frequently, they wouldn't be enticed back but had to be recaptured instead, which would mean I'd have to call for help and spend an hour or so trying to corner them. Similarly, when I needed to get them in to check on their wellbeing, usually once a week, I had to get three or four helpers so we could manoeuvre them from one side of the field to the other. There I'd be like some kind of hopeless commander of infantry, desperately waving my foot soldiers into position, trying to outflank the animals, who would then charge their way through our lines, forcing a retreat and causing the whole operation to be started from scratch.

*

I wasn't short of advice. The choice of Balwens was less than applauded by those in my acquaintance who knew a bit about sheep farming. It wasn't just their jailbreaking tendencies that earned disapproval; they had a more serious complaint. The breed was just too damned small to be viable. Balwens weren't so much sheep as 'rats'. If I was to serve them in the restaurant we'd need to 'give one each'. On top of that they were slow-growing too. Economically they were most farmers' idea of a walking disaster. Wyn was no pushover either. His Balwens were registered with the society which meant that when he got a lamb with all the right markings he could sell it at a show. A lamb like this might fetch as much as £200, nearly ten times as much as the smaller Balwen lambs fetched at market.

All this talk made me question my decision. But then again I was used to

paying more than the average for meat that had a better flavour. In the restaurant, when it was available, we used salt-marsh lamb from nearby Ferryside or the Gower where the sheep graze on sea meadows that are abundant in salt-marsh grasses, samphire and sea lavender. It costs more than most Welsh lamb but it's worth it. I didn't have a salt marsh and I couldn't import one. If I could find a special route to flavour it was going to be in the breed, in this slow-growing, scatty species of Welsh mountain sheep. That was why I was committed to Balwens, and because they're prettier than other sheep.

How much did I contribute to the eventual flavour of the lamb on the plate? Not much. I chose the breed based on a scrap of intelligence about their flavour and the simple fact that they were slow-growing, but more than anything I chose them because I fell for the romantic story of their Tywi Valley origins and the lone surviving ram of 1947. Other than that, it was more about what I didn't do. The land they were raised on is not certified organic, I didn't have the time to make it so, but it was chemical-free and the sheep lived on nothing else but the grass and plants. I guess, with the exception of the times that they were being hunted down for recapture, it was a relatively stress-free existence, and when the time came for them to go to slaughter, their last journey was less than ten miles away. And yet, despite being painfully aware that I could claim little responsibility for its eventual quality, I desperately wanted my lamb to come out on top when we took it to London for the taste test.

It had something to do with taking it to London I suppose. I'd spent a good part of my working life as a food critic there whist my home had been in distant west Wales. In a restaurant like Galvin Bistro de Luxe, run by the brothers Chris and Jeff Galvin whom I knew well, I felt as if it was a little bit of my home country's reputation on the line. Added to that, I was also a big admirer of these two as chefs and as people. As a critic I'd sat in judgement on their food and it had always found great favour with me. Now I was sitting in their latest restaurant, in my opinion one of London's finest, and it was my efforts that were being judged.

So, the excitement you see on screen when the Balwen came out on top is real. As I chose the best lamb from those two plates of *navarin* I had no clue whether it was mine or the product of their usual supplier in Launceston, Cornwall. In fact, with my customary glass-half-empty outlook I assumed it wasn't mine. Both dishes were good, but there was only one winner and given the efforts that those guys go to in sourcing the best produce, it was a notable victory.

It's been enough to convince me that there's something special about the Balwen breed. I kept the ewes and Wyn lent me a ram later in the year, so now we have our own Tywi valley lambs, the first Balwens born on this little patch of Carmarthenshire land.

Hot Pot

Not much more than meat and potatoes, as simple a marriage as can be imagined, but not a relationship that can be hurried. These ingredients need to get to know each other well, slowly warming to each other until the meat is tender and the potatoes are rich with the flavour of the juices. Make sure it's golden brown and crispy on top.

You will need . . .

4 lamb neck fillets	Salt, pepper and flour
1 large onion, thinly sliced	1 litre chicken stock (see page 138)
2 kilos Maris Piper potatoes, thinly sliced	½ kilo carrots thinly sliced
Thyme leaves	Olive oil and butter

Feeds six comfortably or four uncomfortably

Trim the lamb fillets of any sinew and cut into 1 inch pieces then dust these with flour seasoned with a little salt and pepper. Coat the base of a heavy casserole dish (of about 24cm diameter) with olive oil and heat. When the oil is really hot, brown the lamb pieces. You need to do this in a single layer making sure that the oil doesn't cool and removing the pieces from the pot when browned. Now add a little butter, just enough to fry the onions in. Add the thyme leaves and carrot at this point too. When the onions and carrots have softened remove them from the casserole. Layer the lamb, the onion carrot mixture and the potatoes in the same pot, finishing with a thick layer of potatoes. Now add the stock and bring to a boil on the stove. Season well, put the lid on and stick it into the oven at 140°C for 2½ to 3 hours. Take it out and brush the top with melted butter, put it back in the oven, lidless, for fifteen minutes. One green vegetable is all you need with this and buttered leeks or cabbage would be appropriate.

Some say that this dish was first made for the miners of the North-west who took the stone pot, wrapped in blankets to keep it warm, down the pit for their lunch. Others claim the aristocracy invented it for days out at the races. My money's on the miners – food as honest, warming and deliciously simple as this is typical of the resourcefulness that emerged from the kitchens of working people scraping a living.

Roast Loin of Lamb, Moroccan Spices, Beans, Couscous

They do a fair bit of sheep farming in Morocco but there the similarity to West Wales ends. Welsh breeds feed on lush green grass, often on mountainsides, and the need to keep warm accounts for the amount of flavoursome fat you find in the meat. Moroccan sheep spend a lot of the time sunning themselves and their diet is comparatively meagre. As a result most of their fat is stored in the tail and the meat has less depth of flavour than we're used to. That's one reason for spicing things up a little, but in this recipe that Maryann made up for a dinner with friends, the spices are gentle and complementary. This is not about using powerful flavours to disguise poor meat — it's just a case of giving a sweet new accent to something that's already delicious.

For the Lamb you will need . . .

2 loins of lamb, (about 1 kilo) boned and rolled and tied, (get your butcher to do this; if he or she won't, get another butcher)
½ tsp ground ginger, 1 tsp ground paprika and 1 tsp cumin seeds

3 cloves of garlic, 3 sprigs of rosemary
sea salt
pepper
Olive oil

Put all the spices and herbs in a pestle and mortar and crush, add seasoning and enough olive oil to mix it to paste. Score the lamb loin with a sharp knife, rub with the spice mixture and leave to infuse for one hour. Cut the loin in half and roast in the oven at 190°C for 25 minutes. Leave to rest in the roasting tin for 15 minutes. When serving cut into thick slices and drizzle with roasting juices.

For the beans you will need . . .

200g dried beans (some combination of alubia, blackeyed, kidney, haricot) soaked overnight
2 sliced onions

1 whole bulb of garlic, peeled and finely chopped
2 kilos fresh tomatoes roughly chopped
Olive oil

Heat the olive oil in a heavy casserole and then add the onion and garlic. When these are soft, add the beans and fresh tomatoes, stirring well. Add enough water to cover the mixture, bring this to the boil and then season with salt and pepper. Turn the heat down to a simmer and cook for 1½ hours.

For the couscous you will need . . .

½ kilo couscous

50g flaked almonds, toasted in the oven

100g chopped dried apricots

2 bunches of spring onions, washed and finely sliced

1 litre boiling water

1 tblsp olive oil

Salt and pepper

Feeds four in some style

Pour the water onto the couscous and leave for 5 minutes to fluff up. Add the olive oil and stir thoroughly, then add the almonds, apricots and spring onions. Stir well again and season.

Naturally this dish works best if all the bits are finished at the same time. To achieve this, sort the beans out first, then while that's simmering away, deal with the lamb. Do the couscous while the lamb is resting.

Navarin of Lamb

If you saw the programme you'll notice this dish featured on the opening titles as well as in the lamb episode itself. That's because it looked so damned good. People say we eat with our eyes. I say that's a recipe for poking your eye out with a fork and getting a messy face. When I was given this dish for the 'taste test' at the magnificent Galvin Bistro de Luxe Jeff Galvin decided to blindfold me in case I might recognise my own meat (don't go there). It still tasted sublime but I did miss out on the visual beauty of the dish. Not that it was presented with any sort of fanciness. Good food tends to look good anyway without being arranged into ludicrous towers or assembled as a row of bite size titbits on a rectangular plate, with a swoosh of sauce placed at a jaunty angle. The latter is some people's idea of 'modern British cooking.' It's my idea of a bad joke. This isn't the Galvin version but the Polyn version instead. It's a little rougher around the edges but potentially just as delicious.

You will need . . .

12 small whole baby carrots, scrubbed

3 leeks cleaned and cut into half inch chunks

12 shallots peeled and left whole

8 neck chops

1 tbsp tomato purée

1 onion finely chopped

3 cloves of garlic, peeled and finely chopped

3 sprigs rosemary

1 litre chicken stock

Salt, pepper and flour

Olive oil

Butter

Feeds four – that's two chops and three carrots each, plus ¾ of a leek.

Hmmm . . . you might want some mash

Dust the neck chops with seasoned flour and fry in a heavy casserole in a little olive oil until nicely browned. Remove and put to one side. In the same dish fry the onion and garlic until soft and then add the tomato purée and a tablespoon of plain flour together with a tablespoon of butter. Mix all this together to form a paste and then slowly add the stock to make a thickened, smooth sauce. Return the chops to the casserole and bring to a simmer before putting into the oven at 140° C for 1½ hours.

Melt a little butter in a large, heavy frying pan and cook the shallots gently until golden brown. Add a little splash of water to stop them drying out. In a separate pan melt a tablespoon of butter and gently colour the whole carrots for about 5 minutes, adding the leeks for the final 2 minutes. Carefully add the shallots, carrots and leeks to the casserole dish and return to the oven for a further 15 minutes.

Assemble on plates, making sure that everybody gets a pretty equal share of the components. You might want to serve this with some garlic mash but it's not essential.

Devilled Lambs' Kidneys on Sourdough Toast

My wife's not good with offal. I don't mean cooking it — she's good at that, which is weird really, given that she refuses to eat it. Generally I think it's only natural to have a distrust of chefs who cook stuff they won't eat. I once criticised the seasoning of a pretty well known chef's seafood dish and he took me to task over it, didn't agree at all. Later in the argument it transpired he'd never actually tasted it as he had an allergy to fish, so I was the only one of us who knew what the flavour was really like — tough to know where you go with an argument like that. Anyway, Maryann somehow manages to get it right. Instinct, I guess.

For the Lamb you will need . . .

500g lambs' kidneys

Olive oil

Butter

2 cloves of garlic, chopped finely

2 small fresh red chillies, chopped finely

1 glass red wine

150ml double cream

Slices of sourdough bread (see page 132)

Chopped parsley

Feeds 4 as a starter or snack, 2 as a main course or a starter in cases of extreme greed

Rinse and dry the kidneys, cut in half and prepare them by trimming any gristle away and removing the membrane that surrounds them. Heat some oil in a frying pan and add a tablespoon of butter and let it foam. Sizzle the kidneys for about a minute, add the garlic and chilli. Now remove the kidneys and add the wine, cooking until you have reduced the liquid by half. Put the kidneys back in the pan, add the cream with a dash of Worcestershire Sauce and then season. Bring to the boil and cook for a couple more minutes to reduce further.

Slap a good portion on sourdough toast and sprinkle with the parsley.

Rump of Lamb
Garlic, Onion and Thyme Purée

Good word rump. The same cut (from the top rear of the lamb) also gets called chump which has quite different connotations. Rump evokes it best in my view, it's a lean but very ample and tasty cut that you can serve a nice shade of pink. On the subject of rumpy pumpy, Jay Rayner came and reviewed Y Polyn for The Observer and he ate exactly this dish. He said the sauce was so good that he could imagine smearing himself all over with it. I've found it's best not to form a mental picture of that.

Of course, it's always important that you work hard on sourcing the best ingredients you can — that's half the work in all really good cooking but in a dish like this it's of extra importance. This lamb has nowhere to hide. Salt marsh lamb would be ideal.

For the Lamb you will need . . .

4 rumps of lamb (approx 200g each)	6 shallots, peeled and quartered
Olive oil	6 cloves of garlic, peeled and halved
125g salted butter	6 sprigs of thyme
4 large onions, peeled and thickly diced	Salt and pepper

Feeds 4 although you'll need to substantially increase the quantity of the puree
if you intend to use it for smearing purposes

Make the purée. Melt the butter in a heavy pan over a low heat and add the onions, shallots, garlic and the leaves from the thyme. Throw in a good pinch of salt and a grind of pepper. Cook all this slowly for about an hour and a half until the mixture is soft and caramelised, stirring occasionally. Purée the mixture in a processor or using a stick blender, put to one side and reheat when needed.

Season the lamb with salt and pepper. Heat a little olive oil in a pan suitable for the oven and when very hot put in the lamb, skin side down. Sear each side until golden and then return it to the skin-side down position before putting it into an oven at 180°C. Cook for approximately 15 minutes (this should leave it pink). Remove the lamb from the pan, cover with foil and rest for 10 minutes. Slice each rump into approximately 6 pieces and serve with the purée. You might like to serve creamy garlic potatoes with this (see page 136) and if it's the right time of year some very fresh runner beans.

Mark on lamb

" I spent my childhood in my native Scotland, my young adulthood among the heathens in England and, as I enter middle age and its supposed maturity, I find myself raising a family in Wales. Sheep enter the food chain as either lamb, hogget or mutton and I was going to attempt to draw some parallels between my life and the life of a sheep destined for the table, but the geography doesn't really work. When it comes to sheep (all off-colour innuendo aside) the Welsh have the rest of Britain licked.

Welsh mountain lamb is an astonishing product. It is reared on slopes so precipitous that not a lot else can be farmed on them. Once lambing is over, the offspring don't require a lot of other intervention by people and, most importantly, their meat tastes fantastic. It's a product which deserves a place in the worldwide food hall of fame (were such a thing to exist). I knew all of this before I moved to Wales. What I didn't know was that the Welsh have actually trumped themselves and produce an even better lamb than the mountain stuff. Forget your over-pampered Kobe beef or overpriced Bresse chickens: Welsh saltmarsh lamb is a world-beating product. It is reared under very specific conditions on 'sea meadows' which have to be regularly flooded by seawater. The lambs graze on wild herbs and Sparta grass, which results in meat with a flavour which is somehow both more pronounced and more refined than the mountain stuff.

In recent years, much has been made of the so called Mutton Renaissance championed by the Prince of Wales. It's a worthy cause. Many of the characteristics of great lamb are best seen in older animals. We'd love to use more mutton at the restaurant but it is still rather difficult to get hold of regular supplies in the quantities we need.

The farmyard flavour of mature lamb is what I love best about it but I do understand that it can be a bit strong for some people. Perhaps this is why I like our roast rump of lamb dish in preference to the sweeter, more tender (but to me a bit blander) rack of lamb we sometimes serve. That said, I still think that the roast cannon of lamb rolled in herbs and served with a ratatouille jus which I ate at Aubergine (when Gordon Ramsay was still there) for my thirtieth birthday is one of the most delicious things I have ever eaten. **"**

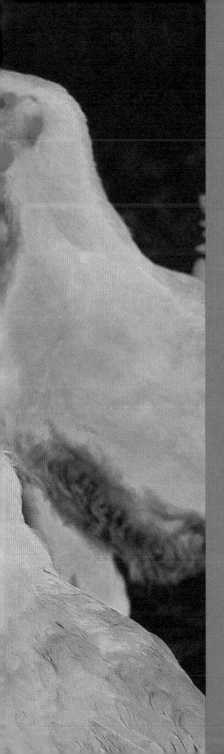

Chicken

As a child, I was surrounded by farmland, but the number of people actively working on the land had already dwindled to a handful. Mechanisation had seen to that. What was left was a family matter with the odd bit of labour hired from outside. For the children, though, it was still a way of life. These kids always struck me as a little set apart from the rest of us – but then, they were being marched to an entirely different tune. Whilst the rest of us rolled out of bed, rubbed the golden sugar from our eyes, stumbled to the table and waited to be fed and watered, they were breakfasting on the cold morning air, stirring the livestock and discharging their own feeding and cleaning responsibilities. By the time they arrived at school they'd put in an hour or two's work. After school it would be the same routine.

Sometimes, when school was over and we played sport, the farm children wouldn't be able to make it because of the chores to be done at home. I knew a few like this and they were old beyond their years. The realities of life had come early and left them with an uncommon gravity and an untouchable solidity – the bullies left them alone. They'd already put away the childish things that consumed the rest of us, or maybe they never got them out to play with in the first place. If this was the way that most people used to live, it made me wonder whether childhood was something that had only recently been invented, at least the kind of easygoing childhood I was living.

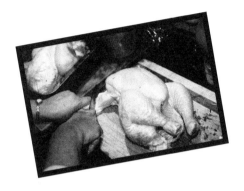

These kids, from toddler days, were on first-name terms with mortality. Birth and death was all around them and they were active participants in the cycle. One day, a rumour went round the playground that Paul Venter killed chickens with his bare hands, Paul was nine years old, lived on a farm with his grandparents and his mother. I never did learn what happened to his dad. Paul was never any trouble, never excelled in class, kept himself to himself. A strong boy who could never see the point in competitive sport, he used to line up next to me in assembly. I remember he sang with real enthusiasm, at the top of his voice. Just a shame he never used any of the right words; instead, a stream of weird sounds and unconnected syllables, like he was singing in tongues. I asked him about it one day, thought it might be an agricultural thing, something they did on the farm. He just looked at me hurt, in a confused way; apparently in his head he was singing just right. I never mentioned it again.

It turned out that Paul did indeed kill chickens for the pot, although I never saw him do it. I did see him demonstrate the method, though, first on a jackdaw with a wounded wing that somebody found at the school gate and secondly on the boy who grassed him up for doing it and caused him to get the slipper. The headmaster was as unconnected to the brutal morality of the countryside as I was.

*

And for many years it seemed that that was as close as I would get to animal husbandry. Largely, I stayed in the country but I floated above it, an ardent admirer. Nature could make my heart race with her beauty and I loved her deeply, but it never got physical – one look at my hands will tell you that. By the time he reached adolescence, Paul Venter must have put hundreds of birds to death with his bare hands. But it was another thirty years before I killed my first chicken.

At the abattoir you're a witness, but you're more than that, more than an accessory even. After all, it's you that's taken the contract out, hired the hitmen, called time on your victim. There's 'blood on your hands' but it's only metaphorical; you're a third party to the actual deed, with someone else as the terminator. That's the way it is these days: almost all killing of livestock for meat is carried out by people who are paid to do it, in carefully controlled conditions. The only real exceptions are where people keep a few poultry for their own consumption or occasionally administer a kind of euthanasia, where the killing is done to prevent future suffering. I was forced, as it happens, down the latter road, a reluctant executioner.

*

The pace of meat production was a shock to me. None of the animals I raised was chosen for rapidity of growth but birth and death often seemed uncomfortably close neighbours. With chickens you seem to have hardly welcomed them and you're saying goodbye. They come into the world such fragile frames, susceptible to the slightest climatic change, easily suffocated by their neighbours and all your efforts are dedicated to keeping them alive. Then, just three months or so later, you have to turn your thoughts to the mechanics of their demise. I found it a wonder that nature does such a good line in fast food, and yet typically, we remain impatient, too greedy to wait. So

we breed and feed in cunning ways until we get it down to 42 days or even less. That way we win the race with nature. But there are losses too: the poultry lose their freedom; their instincts have no place for expression; they exist but don't live. And we lose too: we lose the flavour; we lose the respect for what we are eating and through the way we treat these animals, we lose our dignity. Notables like Hugh Fearnley-Whittingstall have been on this case for a while now. I find it faintly amusing to witness the criticism that these campaigners endure on the grounds of elitism. The argument runs that it's all very well for the middle classes to soothe their troubled consciences by buying only chicken that has at least been given a modicum of respect in its living environment – they can afford it. What about the less wealthy masses that rely on the £2.50 bird to keep starvation at bay? To me it's a weird limp-left argument that says 'think of the poor, feed them crap'. Thirty per cent of the food we buy is wasted: do we really want to encourage that? Or should we be promoting a little bit more respect for what we eat? Most people have enough resources to have at least some choice in the quality of food they eat and for those that don't, isn't it unacceptable that they are that short of money in the first place? That's the problem that needs addressing. It's particularly galling when you hear this stuff spouted by the likes of Jay Rayner, restaurant critic of *The Observer*. Jay is the best of the national critics in my view and, believe me, I thought that even before he wrote a generous review of Y Polyn, but he's gone over to the dark side on this one.

*

I did a fair job of nursing my chickens through their early weeks and there were no fatalities. Just one chick struggled. Only one of its legs seemed to be functioning properly and as it grew, the disability became more pronounced. 'Hopalong' had a splayed leg that jutted out, rigid, parallel to the ground. In

every other respect this bird was the same as all the others. It adapted too, perfecting a curious but effective way of moving by dragging itself around with its one good leg. I read up on the disability and tried to correct the leg by attaching a splint; apparently this sometimes works but it didn't help Hopalong. As the other birds reached maturity, Hopalong's handicap became more obvious. They were outside strutting around the paddock, grubbing up worms, sleeping in the shade whilst he stayed in the shed, physically unable to enjoy the same freedoms. He started to look a sad, tatty and careworn figure and most days I thought about putting an end to his discomfort, but always I left it for tomorrow.

*

We had a different soundman for this stage in the filming: Mike. He'd come down from the Preseli Hills, I think, in his Land Rover that ran on vegetable oil. Mike was a tall oak of a man, a leader in his field; he usually worked on Merchant Ivory films. He had silver locks tied back in a ponytail and there was a presence about him that made you feel he'd seen enough to be sure of his ground. I liked him straight away. We had a good day filming and nearing its end we hauled the equipment over to the chicken shed to pick up some shots as I fed the poultry. Mike spotted Hopalong, picked him up and looked at him plaintively, before setting him back down in the straw. Mike looked straight at me and said softly, 'You gotta kill him, man.' I knew what he was saying and I felt ashamed. Hopalong needed putting out of his misery and I should have dealt with it earlier. Mike went back to his sound duties and I didn't mention anything to the rest of the crew. I knew I'd have to kill him before the day was out and the thought of that was bad enough – without spectators.

*

Mark and I had carried out some research on the chicken question, the question being which breed I should get. There's a fundamental truth about this kind of investigation into the quality of food and that is, that it can't be done without eating. So it was with a heavy heart that Mark joined me in the kitchen of Y Polyn where a steaming row of plates were lined up for our consideration.

You can get used to this kind of treatment. When I first became a restaurant inspector, eating for free was a novelty. Eating out had long been a preoccupation but if the will was there the means were often absent. Applying for the job had been a throw of the dice, an application form thrown into the wind for the hell of it. I nearly didn't bother and I didn't expect anything to come of it. Jobs that involved eating out at someone else's expense and being paid for having an opinion tend to be reasonably popular (I later learnt there were 600 applicants for 4 posts) and I could imagine plenty of better qualified candidates. But there I was, at the table of plenty, menu in hand. The trough was open and there was nobody standing guard. I dived in, and within a year I'd gained a couple of stone in weight. I was like a pig that is being fed at will, like Homer Simpson confronted with infinite doughnuts. But it was worse than that. Even when I didn't want to eat, I felt obliged to. As an inspector, I would 'declare' after every meal, handing in a business card to the manager, letting them know I'd been there and it worried me that they'd read too much into it if I hadn't eaten everything they put in front of me. Consequently, I was expanding at an alarming rate, ballooning at a pace which would have satisfied a factory farmer. It couldn't go on and I developed techniques for secreting large portions of a dish about my person wrapped in napkins or sealed in polythene sandwich bags for later disposal. Later, as my confidence grew, I stopped worrying about the insecurities of the chef and just ate as much or little as I desired. They could read into it what they liked, and they would probably be right. If it was good I was hardly going to leave it.

Mark was a restaurant inspector too, a very good one. His knowledge of food far outstrips mine, he has excellent taste (in other words we usually agree) and his enthusiasm for eating is a wonder to behold. Mark and I watched the final edit of the Chicken episode together on a big screen in the dubbing suite. The taste test appeared on the screen, the pair of us tucking into plates of coq au vin made from different breeds of chicken. I watched as Mark collapsed into a squirming heap beside me, covering his eyes and exclaiming 'I eat like a pig!' I was surprised that this came as a revelation to him; I'd been telling him that for years

If the food is good, Mark eats greedily, bright-eyed and with a smile on his face. It's actually quite endearing. The speed and gusto with which he consumes might suggest he grew up in a large family where he had to fight for his share of the pie. But he's an only child: he just loves food, that's all. As you may have gathered, for me it's something of a love affair. For Mark, it's much more obsessive than that; he's a stalker of gorgeous grub, a pursuer of running buffets, a lunchtime Lothario. And when he goes it'll be in a suicide pact, Mark and his last supper, a smile on his greasy lips, a belly stretched to bursting point, exiting with one last belch.

*

The chicken that came first was from France which was good for two reasons. One, it meant that Mark and I could make a string of poor jokes about not being able to beat 'an expensive French bird', which gave us great pleasure. Secondly it meant that I could buy the day-old chicks from an organic poultry farm just a few miles away where they use the same breed.

Steve Merrit and his wife Juliet moved to this Carmarthenshire smallholding from Wiltshire. They share the land with three children, a smattering of dogs and a large but well-dispersed population of poultry. They're the kind of

independent, self-sufficient people whom I look up to, probably because I know I'd be rubbish at what they do. As well as chickens they keep geese, ducks and turkeys, all of which roam around at will in the meadows that surround them. It's a great place to visit. At a rough guess buying your bird from them will cost you twice as much as the average supermarket specimen, but you could look at it this way:

You drive out into the countryside and after a few wrong turns you locate Llwyncrychyddod farm. Then you bounce along the lane that leads to their house, avoiding the worst of the potholes until you're greeted by a yapping dog and a couple of barking geese. Steve shows you around a few of the poultry houses and your kids get to pet some day-old ducklings before you go to the cold room and pick out a couple of birds for tomorrow's Sunday lunch. The next day you take the time and care to cook them perfectly, the aroma is coming down the hall and the fat is spitting in the oven. You have a long,

slow and delicious family lunch, accompanied by a red wine that gets better by the glass and you're lost in a general feeling of well-being that makes you count your blessings. You look at your glass and are surprised to find that for once it's half full. This has cost you an extra ten to fifteen quid, but never forget, for the same money you could buy yourself one of those self-help books by Paul McKenna or the like and hypnotise yourself into a state of similar reverie.

*

You can hypnotise chickens too. But none of mine seemed to need therapy – with the exception of Hopalong, they did really well. Once they'd been through the tricky incubation bit it was a pleasure to let them out onto the open paddock. Chickens have a lot to say for themselves. As I approached their shed they'd hear me coming and the cacophony would start. I'd open

their door and they'd explode into the daylight, a mass of white feathers with flashes of red coxcomb. They rarely got shut in before dusk and they were usually out again at six in the morning and yet it was as if they had been imprisoned for a month. Feeding them precipitated a further scramble with little scuffles breaking out, nothing serious but a lot of indignant squawking. One or two of the cocks, barrel-chested and military in their bearing, would try and assert their authority but their posturing attracted little interest. Chickens are good entertainment; study a group of them for a little while and you'll find a whole soap opera going on there, little tiffs being played out, unwanted advances being repelled. Give them freedom and they make good use of it. Are they happier than their tightly caged counterparts? I can only guess, but the more I watched them the more the idea of denying them the ability to express their natural instincts seemed unacceptable.

When it was time for the birds to go I had to pack them into crates the night before their final journey. Doing this in the dark means they are comparatively subdued but it didn't feel right. The fact that they were headed for slaughter wasn't troubling me, I felt I'd made that bargain some time ago, but cramming them into the cages, for however short a time, disturbed me. I was used to seeing these birds run free.

*

Stephen Terry is one of the great contemporary British chefs. Those of you who take an interest in culinary pedigrees will know that he emerged from that kitchen crucible of the early 1990s Harvey's in Wandsworth, one of that remarkable team of chefs led by Marco Pierre White, with Gordon Ramsay by his side. These days he has a pub restaurant in Abergavenny called The Hardwick. With Shaun Hill just down the road at The Walnut Tree, this means that two of my culinary heroes are not only working in Wales but within a few

miles of each other. The people of Abergavenny are surely blessed; I truly hope they appreciate it.

The food that Stephen Terry cooks at The Hardwick is a joy. There's nothing overtly complicated about it, it has few bells and whistles, no towers, no swooshes, no foams, no liquid nitrogen. I have no doubt that he could do all that stuff if he so wished – talk to chefs who have shared a kitchen with him and they generally rate him as the best they have worked with – but he chooses not to. And thank heavens for that. Much of that style of cooking is ludicrous, designed to impress other chefs and to furnish Michelin inspectors with the kind of culinary macramé that dominates the higher reaches of their star system. It's the food equivalent of prog rock, endless self-indulgent guitar noodlings and pretentious 'concepts'. It doesn't contribute much more than to burnish the egos of both the people who produce it and those who consider themselves enlightened enough to appreciate it. You might call it 'clever' but I'd call it smart-arse, and intelligence doesn't even enter the picture. There's a line here, of course – fiddly food isn't universally bad and sometimes it's profoundly good. It's just that there are too many mediocre chefs who get carried away with intricate presentation and the search for some mysterious wow factor. It takes confidence to cook simply and not hide behind tricks and gimmicks.

Stephen agreed to cook my chicken for the taste test. I wasn't too confident as I motored up the A40 in the beetle but I was happy enough at the prospect of being fed at The Hardwick – anything else was a bonus. One of the great pleasures of making the programme was the chance to have some of the meat I'd produced cooked by chefs that I so admired. The trouble is that those chefs, almost by definition, are highly selective about the produce that they use, meaning the competition is always going to be stiff.

The dish Stephen prepared was a quite gorgeous feast of the chicken breast and leg, coco beans (a bit like haricot blanc) and morel mushrooms. I hadn't eaten much that day and I spent a lot of time waiting hungrily in the empty restaurant as they filmed in the kitchen. By the time the food arrived I was ravenous and it was all I could do to make a considered assessment of the relative merits of the two dishes. Both were excellent, believe me, but one was a little finer. As it happened, that was mine, which was rewarding, but not quite as rewarding as eating Stephen Terry's food in duplicate.

Coq au Vin

Traditionally this is a way of making the best of chewy old chicken. Never one to miss an open goal, I made a weak joke in the programme about most men having to make the best of a tough old bird as time passes. In the very first edit they cut to a picture of my wife who was in the kitchen at the time. This could have got me into a lot of trouble, I feel. I'd like to make it clear that I don't actually consider her to be old, nor could she be described as tough, in any pejorative sense.

Firstly you will need . . .

8 chicken thighs

4 chicken drumsticks

1 onion, sliced

2 carrots, peeled and cut into chunks

2 celery stalks, cut into chunks

I whole garlic bulb, halved

A few sprigs of thyme

2 bay leaves

2 tablespoons of plain flour

Salt and pepper

1 bottle of red wine

2 tablespoons of olive oil

Marinate the chicken pieces in red wine together with all the vegetables and herbs. Leave this overnight in the fridge. The next day take the chicken and veg out of the marinade and keep the liquid for later use. Sauté the chicken pieces in olive oil until golden brown a few at a time and then place in a casserole dish.

Now sauté the vegetables until soft in the same pan, adding a little more olive oil if necessary. Add two tablespoons of plain flour and stir until combined with the vegetables. Pour in some of the red wine marinade and stir around to make a thick red wine sauce. Add this to the chicken and pour in the rest of the marinade to cover. Season well, bring to the boil on the hob, cover and put into a low oven at 160°C for about an hour.

Now you will need . . .

125g pancetta, thinly sliced

375g small shallots, peeled

375g button chestnut mushrooms

Serves a pair of cocks and a couple of tough old birds

Fry the pancetta until crispy, remove and then cook the mushroom in the same pan – not too long; they should be just cooked. Sauté the shallots in butter carefully until cooked through, soft and lightly coloured.

Take the chicken pieces out of the liquid and keep warm, strain the vegetables out of the sauce using a sieve and push all the juice out of them using a ladle. Put the sauce into a clean pan, add the chicken, pancetta, mushrooms and shallots. Warm if necessary and serve.

My wife Maryann and my son Jamie, both exceedingly tender.

Roast Chicken with Bacon and Herbs

Some dishes offer camouflage for the main ingredient. A tough old bird can hide out in the rich cover of a coq au vin, softened-up by long slow cooking and painted in the deep flavours of wine, herbs and root vegetables. A simple roasting offers no such sanctuary. Of course, proper seasoning, careful cooking and the odd embellishment, like the bacon and herbs used here, will add a layer of polish to the finished dish but its fundamental success will always depend on the qualities of the bird itself. The received wisdom is that a free-range or organic bird will be that bit tougher, especially in the leg. My experience is that there is some truth in this; the price of freedom for the bird is a little extra mastication on the part of the predator. Nothing jaw-aching, though, and what you lose in tenderness you gain in taste.

You will need . . .

1.5 kilo chicken (the best your budget will stretch to)
125g Welsh bacon
125g Welsh salted butter

A handful of thyme, rosemary and flat leaf parsley
Salt and pepper
2tbsp olive oil

Feeds four with nothing left for sandwiches

Chop the bacon into small pieces (try and use some traditionally dry-cured Welsh bacon like that produced by Albert Rees in Carmarthen market. It's salty, creamy with fat, and has little water content). Put the butter in a large bowl, add the bacon, herbs and a grind of black pepper. Mix this until thoroughly combined (if you took the butter straight out of the fridge you're in trouble). Put the chicken on a board and loosen the skin over the breast. Slip your fingers in between the skin and the flesh and push the bacon and herb butter into the cavity, forming an even layer.

Melt the remaining butter and oil in a large frying pan and when spitting hot, place the chicken breast side down in the pan and then brown on all sides. Place the bird breast side up in a roasting tray and season with a little salt before placing in the oven and roasting for 1½ hrs at 190°C. Remove from the oven and leave to rest for 15 minutes before carving.

Chicken Liver Parfait

Cheap but completely gorgeous — a parfait should, as its name suggests, be perfectly smooth and creamy. It's not an uncommon dish but when it's good I still get a thrill out of it. Some people serve it with toasted brioche, but I'd rather the sweetness came courtesy of a good chutney and prefer to have it served with a light crusty bread, toasted of course. Sourdough is ideal.

You will need . . .

500g chicken livers, trimmed

1 onion finely sliced

2 cloves of garlic, finely sliced

1 sprig thyme leaves, finely chopped

35ml brandy

500g unsalted butter

Salt and pepper

Feeds a lot – ten as a starter

Melt 50g of the butter in a frying pan and cook the onion, garlic and thyme over a moderate heat for about ten minutes until soft. Tip the contents into the bowl of a food processor. Then melt another 50g of the butter in the pan and cook the livers half at a time, until browned on the outside but pink in the centre, and season. Put all the livers back in the pan and add the brandy; ignite the alcohol and allow to burn out. Blitz the onion mixture until it is a smooth puree, add the livers and blitz again. Soften the remaining butter and then add ¾ of it into the bowl of the processor and blitz once again until very smooth.

Place a large sieve over a bowl and pour in the mixture, pushing as much of the mixture through as you can – this will take some patience. Season to taste and pour into a loaf tin or terrine. At this point bang the tin sharply on a hard surface to remove any air bubbles. Ladle the remaining butter on top of the parfait, taking care only to use the clarified liquid, leaving behind the milky residue. This will give you a thin layer of clear butter on the surface. Place in the fridge for 2 to 3 hours to set.

Turn out and slice to serve with the aforementioned toast and chutney.

Chicken, Sherry, Canellini Beans and Gremolata

One of those deeply satisfying supper dishes.

You will need . . .

8 chicken thighs, 4 chicken drumsticks
250g cannellini beans
8 garlic cloves
8 bay leaves
100ml dry sherry
1 litre dry cider
Olive oil
Salt and pepper

For the gremolata
Zest of one lemon
25g parsley
1 garlic clove

Feeds . . . do the maths

Soak the beans overnight in plenty of cold water. Fry the chicken pieces in olive oil until golden brown (a few at a time, don't crowd the pan). Place in a casserole dish with the beans, which you will need to have drained and rinsed. Tuck in the bay leaves and peeled whole garlic cloves amongst the chicken. Add the dry sherry and the cider to cover the chicken and the beans. Season, bring up to the boil and cover. Put in a low oven at 160°C for 2 hours until the beans are soft.

Finally chop the parsley, the garlic clove and the zest and mix together to make the gremolata.

Plate up the chicken, one drumstick and two thighs for each person, then pour the beans and the cooking juice over them. Finally sprinkle with a little gremolata.

Chicken and Leek Cobbler

Chicken and leeks have a real affinity and they are at the heart of this dish. A cobbler is basically a dish that is topped with what amounts to scones. They soak up the juices, which is always nice.

You will need . . .

4 chicken breasts, skin removed

6 leeks

500ml chicken stock (see page 138)

250ml cream

Salt and pepper

500g self-raising flour

250g butter

Bunch of chives, finely chopped

100ml milk

1 tbsp salt

1 egg

Feeds . . . it's in four bowls

Chop the chicken into chunks, about 6 pieces per breast. Clean the leeks and cut into ½-inch pieces. Fry the chicken in a flameproof casserole a little at a time in 50g of the butter until it is lightly coloured. Season and return all the chicken to the pan, add the chicken stock and after bringing to the boil, simmer for 20 minutes. Add the leeks and simmer for a further 10 minutes and then add the cream and simmer for a further 10 minutes until the sauce thickens. Put into 4 individual ovenproof bowls and leave to cool.

Make the cobbler mixture.

Oh, you want to know how . . . sieve the flour into a bowl, add the tablespoon of salt. Chop cold butter into small pieces and rub into the flour before adding the chopped chives. Next pour in the cold milk and mix to form a scone mixture. Roll to 2cm thick and using a round cutter, cut into about 12 to 16 circles. Place the overlapping rounds on top of the chicken mixture, three or four on each one, obviously, and brush with beaten egg and milk. Bake in the oven at 200°C for 20 minutes until cobbler mixture is golden brown and risen.

Mark on chicken

"The state of the poultry business has had much press in recent years, with the likes of Hugh Fearnley-Whittingstall and Jamie Oliver flying the flag for proper chooks, but the day-to-day reality is that it's still really hard to avoid poor quality chicken. Chicken, when I was small, was the very best Sunday lunch treat. Admittedly, Mum served it with Colman's packet bread sauce but God, how I loved it. She would have bought the chicken at the local butcher's shop and he, in turn, would have bought it from within a 20-30 mile radius.

We are really lucky here in Carmarthenshire; we have the wonderful Steve Merritt and Juliet Fay from S&J Organics who not only supplied Simon with his chickens but provided me with the tastiest, plumpest goose for Christmas day last year. Visionaries like Steve and Juliet are, however, thin on the ground. It costs a lot of money for one of their chickens. Of course it does. Good chickens take more than twice the 40 days it takes supermarket chickens to be ready for the knife, and time equals flavour. It costs much more to raise one of these superior fowl and we should expect to pay appropriately for them. It's easy to forget, when we are accustomed to buying pappy, water-injected intensively raised birds, that you should need to chew good chicken. When you're cooking a slow braise like Coq au Vin you need that dense muscle to start with so it can slowly tenderise in the wine and impart its meaty essence to the broth. A cotton-woolly cheapo chook will simply fall apart and you might as well chuck out the meat and drink the sauce as soup.

Taking Tesco to task over the welfare of their birds is a laudable idea but the first approach needs to be to the consumer. Attitudes towards meat in general need to change. We need to accept that good meat costs good money – and therefore perhaps it should be a more irregular treat, as once it was, rather than the daily intake of mediocre fare.

Beef

Getting close to a cow has never been something that's worried me, not in the geographical sense. I spent a childhood in the company of cows, a case of peaceful coexistence, sharing the countryside, not bothering each other and not being especially interested in the other's presence – together but not *together*, you might say.

Most of the time, I was just passing through, anyway, and my mind would be on the destination, not on the journey. Fields were shortcuts to me, corner-cutting pathways to the park, friends' houses or the local shop. It would be rare that I didn't encounter a herd somewhere on the way, but it was an unremarkable event that wouldn't cause me to think twice. Cows were just there, like the trees, the grass and five-barred gates.

It was only much later, in retrospect, that the relationship acquired any significance in my mind. I went to the city to work in local government and one day I found myself wandering across fields on the edge of town, looking at a site where someone fancied building houses. I was with a colleague of similar age but greater sporting stature – something of a loudmouth in truth – and we found ourselves sharing the pasture with a few dozen cattle. That was the trigger for my workmate to shoot off, tearing back to the gate, scrambling to safety, out of danger. I didn't get it: there was real fear in his eyes. Sensing the opportunity, I wandered amongst the scattered animals alone, making notes with a studied indifference – stiffened by pride, like a matador or lion-tamer, a man amongst beasts, daring to go where others wouldn't, refusing to be cowed.

They may not have been cows at all. Let me tell you something: this book is on the level. Tempting though it is, I'm not hiding anything; my ignorance is on open display. Of course, how embarrassing that is for me will depend on your relative intelligence on agricultural matters. As I'm writing this, I can't measure that, so it's an odd relationship from my perspective. But here are the parameters as they seem to me – if you're as uninformed as I was at the beginning of this journey then stick with me, we may learn a bit together. Alternatively, if you're steeped in the ways of the countryside or, more dauntingly still, a farmer, then you get to have a laugh at my expense. That's fine too; I can handle the ridicule at this distance.

The whole 'cow' thing starts with picture books as an infant. Maybe, it begins as a 'moo moo,' in ninety per cent of cases there's an intermediary stage of 'moo cow', and then when things start to get serious and everybody's expecting you to get properly literate it's a 'cow', plain and simple. And for some of us there it ends. For the rest of our lives, whenever we see one of those beasts, it's a cow. A lot of the time we're right, as long as they are the ones with udders, the ones that can produce milk, the females of the species. They really are the cows. As for the rest, they're either bulls if they retain their ability to procreate or steers if they've been cruelly deprived of the same. The latter are also called bullocks which is only a change of vowel away from supreme irony given what they've lost – not that a man should dwell on that too much. Never mind the bullocks, that's my approach.

I wasn't confident about any applying any of these terms until I had a need _____ evident to me that I needed to get acquainted with the terminology, so I looked _____ the internet. And there's one more moniker we need to acknowledge: heifer. That's a cow that hasn't given birth yet, or has had only one calf. When you think about it, the females of this species get a bit of a raw deal given the fact that humans tend to use both their names as terms of abuse. That's not something that makes much sense to me; they're beautiful animals – and I should know, I fell in love with two of them. But then again, they were both blokes.

*

It started with a list. I had £1,500 in my pocket and a card in my hand detailing the 50 or so Welsh Black steers that had been submitted for auction. As was the case so often on this project I felt like the innocent abroad, walking down the street in a strange town with 'Take me for all I've got' written on my forehead. Marts of one form or another take place most weeks in the towns of the Tywi valley but despite living there for twenty years, I'd never even thought of going to one. Right then I'd have been happy to keep up the embargo. The thought of wasting 1,500 quid was troubling in itself but the prospect of looking an idiot worried me more.

This was a pedigree Welsh Black sale, meaning that the heritage of every _____ for sale was certified and traceable, and that seemed important to me. Welsh Black cattle _____ ccess story of the last decade or so, the re-emergence of a native breed based on the quality of the beef produced from it. In

comparison with other beef it stands up well, but there are so many other factors involved in good beef production that simply buying Welsh Black cattle isn't any guarantee of success. One animal is not just like any other; its ancestry and what it's been fed will play a big part in determining the quality of its meat. You don't have to take my word for this. In Wales (and well beyond) it's now common to see Welsh Black beef on restaurant and pub menus. That in itself is great, but bear in mind two things. First, it's commonly said to me (and I don't have the statistical evidence for this) that there is significantly more Welsh Black beef sold than is actually produced. Given that it's something of a premium product and there are cheaper alternatives available from places like Brazil, I don't think this should come as any real surprise. Secondly, there's Welsh Black beef and there's Welsh Black beef. How good it is will depend on those factors I've mentioned and another equally important variable – how the meat has been treated after slaughter. Certain cuts, especially those used for steaks, need to be aged if they are going to realise anything like their real potential in terms of flavour. But it's more complicated than that, there's ageing and there's ageing. To be really effective the meat needs to lose water and be exposed to the air, a process called *dry-ageing* which happens under refrigerated conditions with a good circulation of air. So here's a tip. When you pick up one of those supermarket packs that proudly declares 'aged for 21 or 28 days' on the label, bear in mind that unless it says otherwise it's probably spent a large portion of that maturing process in the plastic wrapper you find it in. That way it doesn't lose the 15% or so in weight that happens during dry-ageing, with economic consequences you can work out for yourself.

At the mart I was at step one – trying to find the best beast I could. I'd called for assistance and it had appeared in the whirlwind form of Andrew James, Chief Executive of the Welsh Black Cattle Society and a man who has done as much as anyone to restore the fortunes of the majestic breed of cattle. Andrew is an enthusiast and an optimist, the kind of guy who propels you forward with the hurricane force of his own energy. I don't know anybody else who talks that fast; I guess he must breathe through his skin because there's no way he has time to inhale in the normal fashion. His presence at the sale was a reassurance to me and then came further assistance when he hooked me up with the president of the society, a beef farmer called John Pratt, who

Just one pen of three cattle at the auction had organic status. I wasn't wedded to the idea of getting organic cattle any more than I'm hitched to the notion of organic food. It was taste that I was after, but in my experience there is a link, at least some of the time, between good flavour and organic production. There are some obvious reasons for that – things are left to grow at the right pace for a start, given time to develop flavour – but I think that if there's one reason more than any other that some organic produce tastes better than its non-organic equivalent, it's that the people who produce it are inclined to take more *care* over what they're doing, think a little more about the quality of the end product and a little less about the quantity. I looked at these three cattle and they were by some way the sleekest and most handsome animals in the auction. I guess it was a total layman's perspective (and not for the first time I was taken by the prettiest on show) but it was a judgement with which my adviser, a man of vast experience, concurred.

There was a caveat, though. We wouldn't be alone in identifying these as

with an award for the best group of cattle at the sale. Also, one of the three had been given the title of the best steer of the day. Everything suggested that these cattle were going to reach a premium price, apparently anything up to £850. If they went that high, then they were out of my price range, because I definitely needed to average £750 across the two animals. It was going to be a close call and I didn't really have a fallback plan. Having seen these animals, I'd set my heart on them.

I was glad to have John Pratt by my side as I bid. It was a struggle to keep up with the pace of the auctioneer and sometimes I couldn't tell whether I was leading or not. This first steer was the one that had been named the best at the sale. Somewhere down the front of the crowd was an acquaintance of mine who specialised in organic Welsh Black beef: John James. He's a nice guy, who later gave me some good advice on looking after cattle, but this was about business. As the price rapidly climbed towards £700 I wasn't sure if he knew it was me bidding against him or not. It was just the two of us and from my vantage point at the rear I could see John James raising his finger without hesitation. The bidding went to £760, I raised to 770 and then again to 790. John James topped it at 800 and although I was itching to give it just another £10, the limit had been reached a while back and I let the animal go to John. I was disappointed, and it put the pressure on because I now needed to secure both of the remaining animals. Once again the bidding raced forward over the £700 mark, but this time it stopped abruptly at £720 on my bid. I had my first Welsh Black steer and a little bit of extra cash to expend on the second one. As it transpired that was exactly what I needed. The last steer from the organic pen went to me for £780. I'd spent every penny of the £1500 I came with.

In point of fact I ended up with some loose change left over. The steers came from the farm of Wyn Davies whose organic farm was in Cardiganshire overlooking the sea. After my successful bids he sought me out, shook my hand and handed me some coins. This, I learnt, was the 'luck', a tradition by which the selling farmer gifts a token amount of cash to the purchaser. What's more, Wyn offered to drop the animals off on my land on his way back west.

It seemed obvious to me from the moment we let them out of the trailer that these two steers would relish the open spaces. They had the run of seven acres of varied land, places to shelter, trees to rub against and as much grass as they could consume. I was hoping in some vague way that all of this would contribute to their eventual flavour but I had another card to play too. In

Japan there is a breed of cattle called *wagyu* that produces the world's most expensive beef. These cattle are fed Japanese lager and receive a daily massage which apparently helps to evenly distribute the marbled fat amongst the meat. I planned a scaled-down west Wales version of the treatment for my guys. Steve Smith and Glyn Lenton run the excellent Ffos-y-ffin brewery just a

Left over from the brewing process is a huge amount of rich brewer's grain and I supplemented the cattle's diet with a daily treat of this. As for the massage, well, I gave the animals a firm pat most days.

*

Of all the animals I kept, the closest bond was with these two. I'd promised myself I'd never give any of the stock names but with these two that was a difficult pledge to honour, partly because there were just the two of them and partly because they had such discernible and distinct personalities. I got around it by giving them a different name every day, any famous pairing that came to mind: Stan and Ollie, Fred and Ginger, Ted and Harold, Marks and Spencer, Eric and Ernie and so on. The one that might have stuck? Felix and Oscar I guess, The Odd Couple. One was sociable to the point of apparent

made you understand the full meaning of unrequited. This didn't change for the entire time they were with me.

I could have watched them for hours and sometimes did. They arrived at 600kg and were the best part of 700kg when they left. That's in the region of ninety stone and watching them lumber through the knee-high grass you could sense something of the Jurassic about them. And yet they were supremely graceful and athletic too. One day when I was putting out some brewer's grain one of the steers was on the wrong side of a dividing fence whilst the other stood by me feeding. Despite my encouragement the displaced steer couldn't work out that it needed just a short walk along the barrier to find a way in. Frustration set in and the steer began pawing at the ground, spinning around on the spot and finally from a standing start, not more than a foot away from the barrier, it jumped the four-foot fence, clearing it cleanly. I wished the cameras had been there.

*

Tomorrow would be my first visit to the abattoir. Felix and Oscar would be debutants too; the trouble was, they weren't coming back. They followed me to the gate in their usual fashion, never quite satisfied with what I'd given them I guess, rumbling along a few feet behind me. I shut the gate, turned and began my walk away but I couldn't help but look back. I'd see them again tomorrow but I sensed that this was the point when our relationship changed. I allowed myself to dwell on it a little, sinking into a gentle melancholy, an indulgence I couldn't allow in the morning.

I didn't sleep but it wasn't guilt that kept me tossing and turning. My friend Steve Smythe would be knocking on the door at 5.30 a.m. giving us about 90 minutes to get the cattle into his truck and off to the abattoir for our 7.30 slot. I knew Steve was worried about getting the steers on board because I didn't have a 'crush' or any of the usual equipment to make it happen. I'd just have to rely on their usual willingness to follow me wherever I led. I'd be dependent on their trust in other words, however misplaced.

Sure enough it proved to be a struggle. We started out in near blackness but once they heard me it was easy enough to get the pair towards the gate. They came looming out of the darkness, pitch-black silhouettes emerging from the blue-black distance – lured by the promise of food. There was something about the way they moved that betrayed suspicion, though, the

sudden shake of a head, a snort of cynicism. The camera lights didn't help either and I found myself getting irritated by the presence of the crew. Right then I couldn't have given a toss if we captured it on film or not; nothing seemed important except trying to bring an end to this relationship with some dignity. I could see the concern on Steve's face too as we coaxed and cajoled

charge; we could only tempt them with food and wait until, eventually, with the dawn breaking, they stumbled into their cage. We slammed the metal door behind them and started off on their final journey.

*

Of course I had no right to be distressed. This was my bed, I'd made it. As to the rights and wrongs of it I don't have the answer. All I knew at the time was that I'd made some kind of bargain at the beginning of this road and it wasn't in my power to break it now. So I watched as these two majestic animals were killed, emptied of their life blood and slashed and sliced until they were the beginnings of what we recognise as meat.

And that was it. That *is* it. You either eat meat or you don't and if you do, you're standing at the end of that process, demanding that it happen. It's a

*

Lin Yutang said that if a chicken is killed and then not cooked to perfection then that chicken has died in vain. Lin Yutang was a revered Chinese philosopher of the last century. Shaun Hill is a revered chef of both the last century and the current one. He told me about Lin Yutang and he also cooked me a sirloin steak that was once part of either Felix or Oscar. It was cooked to perfection, and I'm thankful for that.

Sirloin Steak, Red Wine and Shallot Sauce

Of course, you can use any cut of steak you like for this, depending on your allegiance. Personally I'm not a member of the fillet fan-club, although it has plenty of subscribers. Partly I guess that's because it requires very little in the way of mastication and not having to chew is a big plus for some people. Not me; I find in life you have to put a little effort in to get anything worthwhile out. Secondly, fillet is a cut that's visibly free from fat. Well, as we all should know from primary school, fat equals flavour and we have to live with it.

I can't say it too often — the quality of the steak, whatever the breed of cattle, however they were fed, will still ultimately be determined by how the meat has been aged. Dry-ageing lifts the meat into the elite level of flavour, up there in the heavyweight division, mixing with the stars. It's priced accordingly but that's up to you. If you want to consume poor or mediocre steak every few days, be my guest. On the other hand you could treat yourself to something special once in a while and eat something really memorable.

You will need . . .

- 250g beef trim (ask your butcher for this, they'll save it for you)
- 2 garlic bulbs, halved
- 1 bottle red wine
- 1 litre chicken stock
- 75g butter
- Olive oil
- 4 thyme sprigs
- 4 bay leaves
- 100g unsalted butter, chilled
- 20 small shallots, peeled and left whole
- 4 sirloin steaks about 2cm thick

Feeds . . . well it's a steak each, work it out.

Heat the olive oil in a heavy-based saucepan and sear the beef trim until well-browned, then add the garlic and cook for a couple more minutes. Pour in the red wine – now, this doesn't have to be expensive but it does have to be something you'd be prepared to drink (I'm assuming you have some standards) – add the herbs, bring to the boil and then simmer over a medium heat until reduced by half. Add the stock and reduce by half again. This will take about four hours in total but your kitchen will smell great. Strain this through a sieve and retain the liquid.

Melt the butter in a heavy frying pan and cook the shallots until golden brown (about 10 mins). Add ½ litre of the retained liquid gradually to the pan and cook the shallots until soft.

Season the steaks with fresh ground pepper and drizzle with olive oil. Heat a dry, heavy frying pan (either large enough for the 4 steaks or use 2 pans; don't overcrowd) over a high heat until it's smoking hot. Sear the steaks for 2 minutes on one side and 1½ minutes on the other – this will give you medium rare if your steaks are 2cm thick. Remove from the pan, sprinkle with a little sea salt and leave to rest for 5 minutes.

Warm up some red wine sauce and add 3 shallots per steak. Whisk in the remaining cold butter in small chunks whilst gently warming the sauce; this will thicken it and give it a sheen. Plate the rested steaks and pour on the sauce.

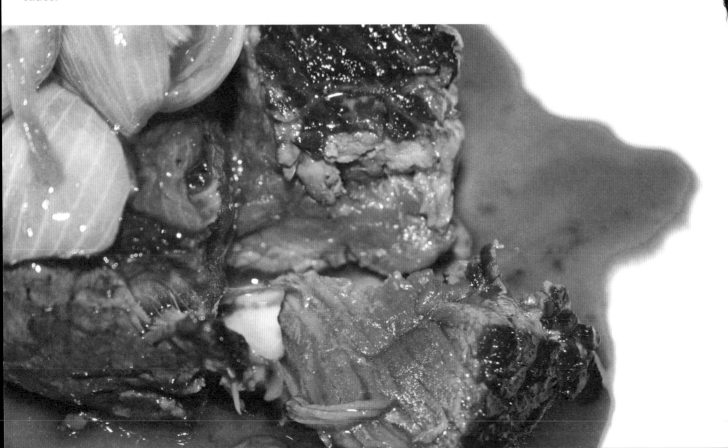

Beef Cheek and Crispy Ox Tongue

Mark came up with this dish whilst lying in bed. Lying in bed thinking about food is a speciality of his and I know few people who do it better. This is a classic case of creating something wonderful out of ingredients that, and it pains me to say this, often get thrown away. It took a bit of selling at first in Y Polyn, because a lot of people were trying these cuts for the first time, but by word of mouth it's become a bit of a cult classic and people actually come in asking for it now. I can understand why — the flavour and texture of the cheek are divine and the crispy tongue is a great contrast. You should be able to make this for less than the price of a supermarket sandwich per person.

For the beef cheeks you will need . . .

4 beef cheeks (about 375g in weight each)	10 black peppercorns
2 carrots, peeled and cut into chunks	Salt and pepper
1 large onion peeled and quartered	Olive oil
4 sticks celery cut into chunks	1 bottle of red wine
4 bay leaves	Butter

Trim the cheeks, removing membrane and excess fat until you are left with lean pieces of fleshy meat. Tie these up into neat parcels using 2 or 3 pieces of string and then marinade in the wine with the vegetables and herbs overnight in the fridge. The next day sear the meat in olive oil until browned and place in a heavy casserole dish. Tuck the marinated vegetables around the meat and season well. Pour in the marinade wine and top up with more red wine to cover if necessary. Bring this to the boil, cover and place in a low oven at 140°C for at least 4 hours, checking liquid every hour to make sure the meat is still submerged (add a little water if necessary). Remove from the oven and leave to cool in the liquid with the lid off. Strain to discard the vegetables and reserve the liquid; take the string off the meat. When ready to serve, heat the meat in half the liquid and put back into a low oven for 20 minutes.

Make the red wine sauce by bringing the rest of the liquid to the boil, whisking in about 25g of butter in small chunks to thicken. Pour over the meat parcels when glossy and thick.

Meanwhile, with your other hand make the **crispy ox tongue**.

You will need . . .

1 small tongue (about 500g)	Duck fat
Salt and pepper	1 egg
Thyme leaves	Panko Japanese breadcrumbs*

Feeds Four

* Panko are royalty in breadcrumb terms. They are larger and lighter than normal breadcrumbs and hence crisp better when fried. They're pretty widely available now but if you struggle to get them, simply use breadcrumbs made from a good quality, open-textured white bread.

Mix together a generous amount of salt and pepper with the thyme and coat the tongue with the mix. Leave overnight in the fridge. The next day melt the duck fat in a saucepan, wipe the tongue clean of salt and place in a small roasting tray so it's a snug fit. Pour over the duck fat to completely cover the tongue and then seal with a sheet of baking paper and a final sheet of foil. Cook this in a low oven at 130°C for 3 hours (the fat must not boil). Leave to cool and then remove the tongue from the fat and chill in the fridge. After 30 minutes or so remove the outer skin from the tongue and cut it into chunks about 2cm thick. Coat in beaten egg and panko breadcrumbs.

When the cheeks are ready to go, deep fry the pieces of tongue at 180 C for around 3 minutes (at this temperature a piece of bread dropped in will sizzle and brown in 30 seconds). Add the golden cubes of tongue to the beef dish.

This is an intensely flavoured dish so you might want to serve some creamy mash to calm things down a bit.

Carpaccio of Beef

Vittore Carpaccio was a Venetian painter of the 15th and 16th centuries. Some of his most famous paintings were heavy on the use of pink, which is how this dish of a similar hue came to be named after him in the 1950s. It was famously invented at Harry's Bar for the countess Amalia Nani Mocenigo, whose doctor had told her to eat only raw meat. One can only guess at her complaint.

Raw meat's not something we're culturally too comfortable with, but here it is thin, delicate and made from that most refined of cuts, the fillet. Once again, using dry-aged beef will take the dish up a division.

You will need . . .

250g Welsh Black beef fillet	A good virgin olive oil
Flakes of sea salt	Baby capers and gherkins
Black pepper	2oz thinly shaved parmesan

Feeds a countess and three friends for a light lunch or as a starter.

Trim any excess fat off the fillet, then you need to chill the beef to make it firm enough to cut or you'll end up with soggy strips of meat and expensive mess. In fact you can stick it in the freezer for an hour and kind of semi-freeze it. Now you need a sharp knife, a really sharp one that allows you to slice the beef about 2mm thick. Now place 3 to 4 slices at a time on a piece of lightly-oiled parchment then cover with another piece of oiled film. Firmly roll the meat out until it is paper thin. Arrange a few slices on each plate and season with a grind of pepper and some flakes of sea salt, drizzle with a little olive oil (this is an occasion to get the good stuff out) and then garnish with parmesan, the baby capers and some sliced gherkin.

You might want to serve this with a rocket salad and focaccia.

Welsh Black Rib of Beef 'Ray Gravell'

If there was ever a special occasion, something to celebrate, throw your hat in the air and forget about your cares dish, this is it. Essentially what you've got is a monster of a steak cut from the middle of the rib joint – and there are those that say it's the tastiest cut you will get. You can serve it with whatever accompaniment you want but the meat will always take centre stage, lead vocal and guitar solos – everything else is strictly rhythm. I'd go for thin chips cooked in duck fat ideally, with a simple béarnaise on the side, but you could easily substitute the red wine and shallot sauce used for the sirloin on page 74.

This dish, commonly known as 'côte de boeuf' is the one that I'd planned to use for the first cooking of the meat of those two magnificent Welsh Black cattle – could there have been any other? It didn't turn out that way, though. I was going to share the occasion with my late friend and hero Ray Gravell who had seemingly just got over the illness that saw him lose a leg. Ray loved his food and I can easily imagine the rapturous reaction Ray would have given to the arrival of this great hunk of gorgeous beef at the table. That very thought brings him back to me in all his raging glory – so this is his dish now.

For the beef you will need . . .

1kilo bone in Welsh Black rib steak (dry-aged naturally)	Salt and pepper
	Olive oil

Season the beef with salt and pepper and drizzle all over with olive oil. Sear the rib an all sides in a heavy frying pan (one that is suitable for the oven) until well crusted on all sides (that means the thin edges too). Stick the pan into a hot oven at 200°C for about 15 minutes (this will give you medium rare). Take out the meat, cover with foil and rest on a board for another 15 minutes. Slice thickly and serve with the béarnaise which you will have finished preparing just a few minutes earlier . . .

For the béarnaise you will need . . .

100ml white wine vinegar

2 shallots finely chopped

2 sprigs tarragon (one finally chopped)

1 tsp course cracked pepper

250g unsalted butter

4 egg yolks

Feeds four normal human beings or one rugby legend and a greedy food writer

Combine the vinegar, chopped shallots, pepper and the whole sprig of tarragon in a small saucepan. Bring this to the boil and then reduce by half before letting it cool. Melt the butter until liquid and put the egg yolks in a heatproof glass bowl over a pan of simmering water. Whisk the tarragon vinegar reduction into the eggs until the mixture turns slightly foamy. Now . . . slowly . . . a tablespoon at a time add melted butter continually whisking until this mixture becomes thick and creamy. If at any time the mixture starts to curdle take it off the heat and add a few drops of cold water and whisk again. Add the finely chopped tarragon and season with freshly ground pepper and salt.

Daube of Beef, Herb Dumplings

This is a simple French stew bolstered by the addition of some traditional British dumplings, nothing complicated or pretentious about it but a mighty dish nevertheless. The cut of meat is important here: anything too lean and refined will be a terrible waste, because it will just dry out. You need something like chuck which is good news because in relative terms it's cheap too. You need a rich red wine for this and a decent sturdy Cotes du Rhone will be perfect both for the saucing and for drinking with the stew. I guess it's a winter dish but I don't subscribe to that type of perverse seasonalism. I'd eat this any time.

For the daube you will need . . .

1 kilo chuck steak in 2-inch chunks
Salt and pepper
4 onions roughly chopped
4 carrots also roughly chopped
4 sticks celery, you guessed it

2 tbsp flour
Olive oil
Thyme and bay leaves
1 bottle red wine

Sear the pieces of beef in a heavy casserole dish in olive oil until browned on all sides. Remove and put to one side. Add a little more olive oil and add the onions, stirring to colour well. When soft add the flour and combine with the onions then, slowly, add a quarter of the red wine stirring all the time and making a thick sauce. Next return the meat to the dish and add the carrots, celery, garlic and herbs. Give this a good stir and add the rest of the wine and a little water if necessary to cover the meat. Season then bring to the boil before placing in a low oven for at least 2½ hours, checking every hour that there is plenty of liquid (add water if necessary). You're not going to eat this the same day, so put it in the fridge when cool and heat up the next day when the flavours have become properly acquainted.

For the herb dumplings you will need . . .

1 tbsp chopped chives

1 tbsp chopped parsley

150g plain flour

150g white breadcrumbs

150g suet

Salt and pepper

2 egg yolks

Feeds four

Mix the dry ingredients together lightly. Whisk the eggs in a separate bowl and season. Lightly fold the eggs into the dry mixture (using your fingers is best). The dumplings need to hold together so add a little water if necessary to make a light dough, but don't get it too sticky. Form into little dumpling balls, about 12.

Reheat the daube, pop the dumplings into the simmering liquid so they are sort of half submerged. Put the lid on the casserole and cook gently for a good twenty minutes at medium temperature (180°C).

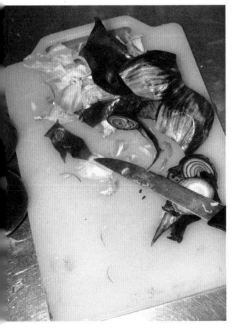
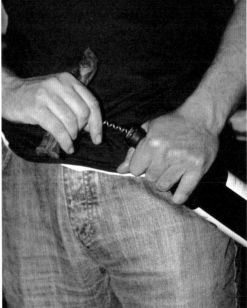

Mark on beef

"
Beef; now there's a subject to stir the most coldhearted of diners. The most delicious steak ever. The most tender and succulent beef stew. The most satisfying and deeply nourishing Sunday roast. Beef really is an emotive thing.

Memories of beef dinners we have eaten reach to us all from childhood – and so very often, Mum's is best. I think my own earliest memories of eating are bound up with beef; my mother used to make a boiled beef and carrots dish which still makes me salivate thirty years later.

I've been really lucky to have eaten at some of the most inspiring restaurants across the globe. I've eaten beer-fed and hand-massaged Japanese wagyu beef in Tokyo. I've chowed down on one of Peter Luger's sensational porterhouse steaks in New York. And I've licked clean the remains of one of Mum's Sunday lunches. I guess I don't need to tell you again which plucks most strongly on my culinary heartstrings.

A great steak is a truly great thing. It can, however, mean many things to peoples across the world. In France, they expect you to chew. Steaks are a bit tougher and the pleasure of mastication is an intrinsic part of the experience. In

Japan, the perfect steak is buttery tender and needs merely the lightest of touches in the mouth. The grain-finished beef in the States is tender but prolonged dry-aging means that the tenderness is tempered by an extreme beefy flavour, often with a strong, blue-cheesy note.

While I love to eat steak, the best expression of beef for me comes when it is slow-cooked to spoonable tenderness. Heston's Blumenthal's oxtail and kidney pudding, which he serves at his pub The Hind's Head in Bray, is an amazing creation. The meaty notes are enhanced with some star anise, the flavouring being the product of this culinary wizard's famous research. I also fondly remember eating a braised brisket dish scented with orange when I worked in Belgravia in London, prepared by the Chinese chefs at Jenny Lo's Tea Shop.

Now while I live and work in Wales, and have a passionate advocate for Wales in my friend and business partner Simon Wright, the Scotsman in me is still certain that Aberdeen Angus is the breed of choice for great beef. I love Welsh Black beef and we use it exclusively in the restaurant. If you were to sit me down at a blind tasting and asked me to compare it to Angus . . . I'm not absolutely sure I would win, but my romantic self would still like to believe it is best. "

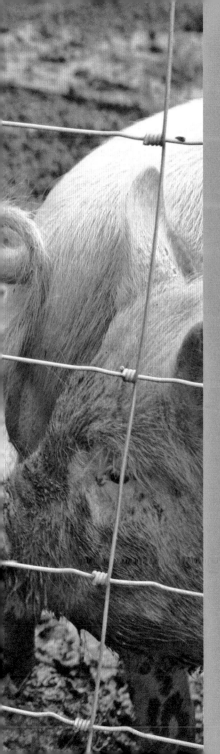

Pork

You have to hand it to pigs: they're serious about food.

I concede that nourishment is a priority for all species but it's the fanaticism of pigs that puts them in a different category. Take sheep for example; they like to eat too, but they graze in a wary and disinterested manner. After all, they know from experience that the grass will still be there tomorrow and for them there are no set mealtimes as such; every waking moment there's a buffet to be found at their feet – you can hardly blame them for failing to get excited about it. In fact, as someone who once ate out for a living, I can entirely sympathise: the novelty does wear off.

As for poultry, they get pretty excited at the prospect of a meal, but for them it's more about the battle than the spoils of victory. Throw them some grain and they're like angry shoppers on the first day of a sale, fighting over a pile of dubious jumpers. When they get one, they will probably never wear the thing, but they're sure as hell not going to let anyone else get it. I swear that chickens take pleasure in bickering, and they do a magnificent line in righteous indignation. We humans can get rightly down on ourselves for our capacity to start pointless wars over lines on maps and discrepancies in religious texts. Don't imagine we're the only bad-tempered species on the planet, though. The only reason that chickens escape the same kind of censorship is because they lack the armaments; if poultry had nuclear weapons the planet would have been cinders long ago, obliterated over a handful of corn.

Like the sheep, my cattle were grazers, though I supplemented their diet with brewer's grain from our local Ffos-y-Ffin brewery. I had a hunch that they might like it and I wasn't wrong. But I guess it was something else that brought me and the steers closer together, like our shared views on politics and the way forward for Welsh rugby – matters which I discussed with them often and at length, with never a word of dissent. Our taste in beer was similarly in tune and although we didn't actually visit the pub together, we supped from the same barrel. The cattle were enthusiastic about the grain; the sight of it would unfailingly bring them to their feet. On a good day, I could get them to traipse across the length of two fields following me as I swung a bucket of it. On a very good day the mere sight of the bucket would have one of them careering towards me like a furry black brontosaurus, coming to a dramatic double-hoofed stop just inches in front of me. Other days, they were hardly interested. After all, some days you need a pint more than others.

Pigs are nothing like as fickle. They're dedicated troughers, trenchermen. Mankind, we fuss and fret about the nature of the universe, bewildered by the meaning of it all, constantly asking ourselves is there really any point? Pigs laugh in the face of the uncertainty of existence. They *know* what the point is; it's in front of them, waiting to be eaten, and when it's not in front of them the answer is just as obvious – they sleep. They take a temporary death, the perfect way to pass the meaningless time between meals. Watch a pig eat, no, *listen* to a pig eat. Now, you can kid yourself all you want, but those grunts are the most satisfied noises you are *ever* going to hear.

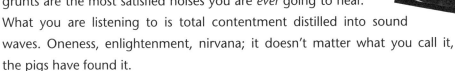

What you are listening to is total contentment distilled into sound waves. Oneness, enlightenment, nirvana; it doesn't matter what you call it, the pigs have found it.

*

Whilst I don't live to eat in the way of the pig, it's no secret that I take pleasure in my repast and I suppose, sometimes, it might be described as good for the soul. When something tastes really great, well you might argue that it approaches the spiritual at times, in the same way you can make a similar case for music or visual art. I've often wondered what it is that makes one food taste appealing and another abhorrent. There are answers to those questions apparently, the usual stuff relating to the need to be attracted to those things that will sustain us and our species. Sugar's pretty important to our existence in one form or another and most of us are partial to something sweet now and again, so it all works out in a happy way. Clearly it's not been perfected, though. Maybe, if we give ourselves the chance, we will evolve into a species that perfectly balances our appetites with our physical need for nourishment. My experience tells me we currently have some way to go. I want far too much of things that aren't good for me. Beer and wine are the most obvious examples. Middle White pork is another.

I first took real notice of rare breed pork doing my rounds for the AA. Up until that point, pig meat had been well down in my league of carnivorous choices, lagging behind beef, lamb, most poultry and game. In fact, pork was languishing at the bottom of the table, fighting it out with the lamentable turkey, sharing the same miserable characteristics – white, dry and uninteresting. What I later found is that it can be as wonderfully good as it can be miserably bad.

The reaction we get in the restaurant when we serve Middle White pork in particular is telling. The older generation tend to say it reminds them of the pork they occasionally had in their childhood, with a taste they haven't experienced for years. Others simply say they've never experienced pork like it. There's a richness and depth of flavour that you can't ignore; it's seductive to the point that once it has got you in its clutches you'll lose the will to resist. It's the kind of food that can make you eat far more then you really need, too, and have you creeping back to the fridge for leftovers only an hour after you filled your belly with it. It's a porcine triumph – and for me it took on frontrunner status some time ago now, and shows no signs of returning to the pack.

So, in my meat-rearing endeavours, if I was going to produce pork, it had to be Middle White.

*

At Y Polyn we buy our pork (when we don't have a supply of our own) from Richard Vaughan at Huntsham Farm near Hereford (you'll find his details in the recipe section at the end of this chapter). Richard has a lot of Middle White pigs and supplies some of Britain's top restaurants, including guys like Heston Blumenthal. So it seemed the natural place to go to buy some weaners – those just old enough to leave their mothers. I rang him up and asked if maybe I

could have half a dozen piglets. As I understood it, he had over 300 Middle White sows and with litters of around 10 each it didn't seem to me that he'd miss half-a-dozen. I didn't get them. Instead I secured a simple lesson in the economics of farming. Richard's big investment was in the mothers. The sows are the ones that cost the money to keep; they're a permanent fixture. The life of the pigs that will be sold for pork is necessarily short and as a consequence the cost of keeping them is much less significant. So, by the time they're born, Richard argued, the majority of the outlay has been made – he could sell me some, but at a price that would make no economic sense. I could see his point but it was disappointing nevertheless. A rare breed is exactly what the name suggests and I wasn't too sure where to look for an alternative source of animals.

Luckily, I didn't have to look too far. A friend put the word out in the local pig-farming community and was pointed in the direction of Whitland, less than 20 miles west of me. Amanda Windsor keeps Middle Whites there in a gorgeous part of the Taf valley, among a group of whitewashed farm buildings set in still countryside – gently rolling fields, lush and bright, giving way to the dark green crevice that conceals the railway line and the river at the foot of wooded slopes. In one of the outbuildings, we found the sow, the size and shape of a dirigible, and at her side, aligned like chipolatas just unwrapped, a sequence of 11 piglets, tiny, pink and cute to the point of cliché, as if they were models for the archetypal piggybank. The sow, whiskered and frothing at the lip, eyed me with mistrust. Amanda told me she was a good mother; I didn't doubt it. She looked a little tired of the responsibility of feeding and protecting her near dozen offspring, but she also looked as if she'd give her dying breath to protect them. There was something beautiful about that, but generally Middle Whites aren't conventionally attractive in their looks. The snout stops short as if it's been smashed like the nose of a boxer on the canvas, or the result of careering down a hill at full tilt and failing to see the

brick wall at the bottom until it's far too late. This breed has a concertinaed proboscis that dominates the features – and the piglets are born with it, without exception. Never mind, their mother loves them.

*

Actually, they're not hard to love. When we got them home they lay in their arc, fresh-fleshed and squeezed-up in the golden virgin straw, seeking comfort in their siblings. I'd been advised to keep them penned into the arc for three days, so they might adjust to their new surroundings and their sudden orphan status. But the sun was shining and their paddock looked like an impatient Eden. I lifted the board that defined their prison and moved to one side to give them a clean break from the traps. They remained in the corner, peeking out from the straw, bright-eyed and eager but not yet convinced. I left them to it; I sensed these were steps they would take at their own pace.

*

Nature wasn't looking for cheap laughs with those noses. They're a design feature of the Middle White that enables it to root around with an effectiveness denied to others of the species. The flattening of the snout is designed so there is a slight lip at the top of the nose that operates as a little shovel, able to cut into the soil and turn the earth over. Now this appendage isn't big; the diameter of the nose when full grown is no bigger than the petrol cap on your car, and naturally the younger the pig the smaller it is. Nevertheless, five piglets of a couple of months old can turn over a third of an acre in about two weeks if the ground is soft. When they entered that paddock it was grassy meadow; a fortnight later, it was Glastonbury.

This, I think, is where the pig's reputation for being a mucky animal comes from because in all other respects its housekeeping is of the highest order. Their arc, for instance, was always clean and dry; I'd imagined daily rituals of mucking out and I guess that must be the case where the animals are confined indoors, but these pigs weren't about to soil their own doorstep. They allocated a particular section of the land for waste disposal and pretty much stuck to it, while the arc remained pristine – you'd almost call them house-proud. Some mornings I half-expected to find they'd built shelves, put pictures on the wall, ordered a flat-screen telly off the internet.

As the summer went on, the pigs fattened nicely. I was feeding them on a mix of left-over brewer's grain, some commercial feed and, as the autumn came, an increasing amount of apples from my friend Dorian in Nantgaredig village. There was no particular science to this; I just tried to feed them the best food that I could and it was an annoyance to me that they preferred the commercial feed to the brewer's grain – they'd eat it, of course, but not with the relish that they reserved for the stuff that cost me five or six quid a sack. But it was the apples they loved best, and when there weren't any available I was tempted to buy them instead, but the cost of feed was burden enough as it was; pigs eat a lot and quality feed is increasingly expensive. It helps if you can buy in bulk but I had neither the number of pigs to justify it nor the buildings in which to store it. So I persisted with my ad hoc combination and hoped for the best. As was their nature, they rooted around too, grubbing up what little titbits they could find in the rich soil of their paddock.

I couldn't be sure what effect any of this would have on the eventual flavour of their meat. I was convinced I had the right breed and their conditions were as stress-free as I could imagine but the contribution of their diet to the eventual quality of the meat was bound to be crucial. I just hoped the apples and the beer grain were having the right effect. In terms of their physical progress it was obvious there wasn't a problem. They put on weight at an exponential rate, on course for that 50-kilo point which, I had discerned from books and the web, was the ideal weight for a Middle White to be dispatched if used for pork. The wisdom is that for pork you don't keep the animal too long, whereas for bacon, or curing for ham, you let them grow somewhat bigger. I had no real idea how big a 50-kilo pig is. I tried picking one up and it was a struggle, not least because the animal was less then keen on being cuddled. A bag of feed was 25 kilos: were they twice as heavy as that? After six months I began to think they were approaching that mark but wanted to be sure.

*

Throughout this whole farming escapade, friends in the village had been really helpful, none more so than our local doctor, Anthony Davies. Doc is from farming stock and, I think it's no real secret, is a frustrated farmer. As it happens, he's an outstanding GP too, and recognised in the community as such. My guess is that one day they may have to let him go wandering off into the fields in search of his heart. That hasn't happened yet but I think over the past year I benefited from his yearnings. I only had to call and he'd be there, chasing escaped sheep, fixing fences and, in this case, weighing pigs. Doc borrowed some contraption specifically designed for the purpose and once we'd harnessed the porkers, the dial indicated that they were all within a few kilos of their optimum weight.

It made sense for the pigs to depart in stages. A whole pig provides a lot of meat and there was a limit to the amount we could sell through the restaurant. On the other hand, the journey to the abattoir required a bit of organising and It seemed wasteful to take one pig at a time. I also thought

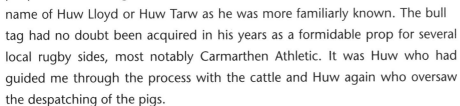

that it would be less stressful if they travelled with some company, so I took the two biggest animals. Thankfully the journey was a short one anyway, just 15 minutes or so, and when we arrived the pigs seemed unruffled. A little reluctant to depart the trailer perhaps, but there seemed no sense of trepidation as they strolled up the ramp into the building that would see their end. By this time I'd already witnessed the death of the two cattle. I wouldn't say it had hardened me but I was familiar with the building, the routine, the people. Chief amongst the latter was a character by the name of Huw Lloyd or Huw Tarw as he was more familiarly known. The bull tag had no doubt been acquired in his years as a formidable prop for several local rugby sides, most notably Carmarthen Athletic. It was Huw who had guided me through the process with the cattle and Huw again who oversaw the despatching of the pigs.

This time I knew what to expect. Somebody had told me there'd be more noise with a pig but I didn't hear anything and in seconds the bodies were lifeless and being tossed into a hot water bath that would help remove their hair, a process completed by a scalping with a razor-sharp knife. I stood with Huw and watched as the innards were removed. One thing I knew for sure was that very little of this animal was going to go to waste. I asked Huw if he'd ever eaten pig's ears and he hadn't. That was a surprise – and it occurred to me at once that I might help rectify that. Maybe I could invite him to come and share some of the pork with us and perhaps it would be good to invite Amanda Windsor, too – she who brought the pigs into the world and he who arranged their exit. Midwife and executioner.

*

A few days later I wound up into the hills above Llandovery, heading for Llanwrtyd Wells and the kitchen of Maryanne Gilchrist.

Maryanne had entered my consciousness many years before when I was running a restaurant near Carmarthen with my wife and her sister. We'd been a fixture in *The Good Food Guide* for quite a few years and it brought us a fair bit of trade. Our score in the guide had remained fixed at 3 for many years and although that might not seem a lot when the maximum was 10, we felt it was an achievement just to be included; we were one of just a handful of featured restaurants across south Wales and few outscored us. One year the guide arrived with a new entry. Carlton House was just 30 odd miles from us and it blasted into the guide with a score of 6, a rating that put the place up there with the Michelin-starred restaurants of the UK, and it wasn't too long before Michelin bestowed that award upon it as well.

As it transpired, I soon ended up at Carlton House on behalf of another guidebook, the *AA Restaurant Guide*. AA inspections were carried out anonymously although it wasn't uncommon to be spotted. Restaurateurs tend to be alert to that kind of thing and a lone diner tends to ring alarm bells amongst the staff, especially at a small hotel in the countryside where business guests are a rarity. Mostly this results in an uncomfortable stand-off. They know who you are but feel they shouldn't say anything and often you know that they know, but have no real choice but to go along with the pretence. Maryanne Gilchrist is not the type to be bothered with an elaborate charade of this type; she waited until I'd eaten and then made it quite clear that she knew exactly who I was. As an inspector I was diligent about keeping my distance from those whose restaurants I was judging – the difficulties one could otherwise get into are obvious. In this case I ended up breaking every rule in the inspector's book, sitting up into the early hours of the morning, drinking whisky and gossiping about the restaurant trade – I promise you, I tried to resist, but Maryanne is a force of nature, a hurricane-strength personality. I guess if I'd had any doubts about her rating then it would have been more problematic, but the food she'd served me was out of the top drawer and I could only concur with the other guides.

*

I knew Maryanne's pork would be out of the top drawer too. She has a reputation for sourcing the best and I wouldn't like to be in the shoes of any supplier who let her down on the quality of produce. It is something she has always taken great pride in, so maybe there was a little extra edge in this particular challenge – she really didn't want her meat to come second to mine. I think it was with this in mind that she devised a very strong sauce to go with the belly pork that she used for her dish. Something with an oriental edge, dark, treacly and strong enough to hamper the taste buds in distinguishing one piece of meat from the other. As it turned out, there was a clear winner. One serving of pork was significantly moister than the other and there was a little more flavour too. I was pretty sure that this must be the meat from her supplier – my reasoning being that my pigs had been given an unusual amount of freedom and hence exercise. Exercise means muscles that have been worked more, and this usually equates to tougher meat. Although I was convinced it wasn't the fruit of my labours, I declared in favour of the better dish. After all, that was my role as a critic: simply to distinguish the best.

That it turned out to be mine was a surprise to me and, I think, to Maryanne Gilchrist. Over the next few months we had an ample supply of our own Middle White pork at Y Polyn and I've raised more weaners since then. Good pork is, to my mind, the finest of meats and this was some of the best I'd ever tasted.

Crispy Belly Pork, Caramelised Apples

Pork belly is one of those cuts of meat that came in from the culinary cold a few years ago and shows no sign of slipping in popularity. There are many reasons to celebrate it: the amber crackling that, done properly, should be light and explosive, the moist melting texture of the meat and that rich, full, porky flavour. The question we get asked in the restaurant is, 'Is it fatty?' There's only one honest answer – yes. As I said in an earlier recipe, fat equals flavour and that's something we have to live with. I sometimes wonder what it would be like to live in a world where these simple pleasures didn't have their downsides. Imagine if beer was good for us . . .

You will need . . .

1 whole pork belly, boned and trimmed
2 whole garlic bulbs, halved
4 sprigs of sage
1 tblsp olive oil
Salt and pepper

1 litre dry cider
8 Granny Smith apples
60g butter
125g caster sugar

Feeds . . . this is the perfect dish for a large Sunday lunch.
One pig's belly should satisfy at least eight human bellies.

In a large roasting tray, scatter the sage leaves, salt and pepper, olive oil and garlic halves. Place pork belly in the tray skin-side up, season and drizzle with a little more olive oil. Pour in ½ litre of dry cider around the pork and cover with baking paper and then foil. Check every 30 minutes and add more cider if it is drying up. Roast in the oven for 2 hours at 160°C. Remove from the oven, uncover and return to the oven at 190°C to crisp up for 30 minutes. Lift the pork into a clean tray and leave to rest for 20 minutes. Now place the original roasting tray on a low heat and add the remaining cider. Bring this up to the boil and then pour into a saucepan through a sieve to collect the garlic and sage. Simmer this liquid until reduced by a third.

While all this is going on, find time to peel and core the apples and cut them into quarters. Melt the butter over a medium heat, add the apples and coat in the butter. Sprinkle the sugar over them and turn the heat up, cooking until the apples caramelise.

Cut the pork into eighths. To get a really good crackling, put the pieces under a blazing hot grill for a short period (don't take your eyes off them or you'll find they've burned). Slice the portions into thick chunks and serve with the sauce and the caramelised apples.

Pork Chops 'Charcuterie'

I imagine this sauce got its name because of the gherkins, a classic accompaniment to much charcuterie. I hear some people don't like gherkins. This is something I find hard to swallow, unlike gherkins which I could eat by the jar were I not conscious that they will later have their revenge. This is a deeply savoury dish and the sauce is addictive but it doesn't kill the flavour of the pork either.

You will need . . .

4 large pork chops, something good like
   Middle White, ideally

1 tbsp olive oil

1 tbsp butter

Salt and pepper

4 shallots, finely chopped

120ml dry white wine

1tsp plain flour

200ml chicken stock (see page xxx)

2 tbsp Dijon mustard

12 gherkins, finely chopped

1 tbsp flat leaf parsley, finely chopped

Feeds . . . depends on how many pork chops you can eat.

In a heavy frying pan suitable for the oven, melt the butter and the oil. Season the chops and sear for 3-5 minutes on each side until nicely coloured. Place in a hot oven at 190°C for a further 10 minutes. Remove from the oven and place the chops on a clean plate to rest, covered in foil. Return the pan to the heat and cook the shallots until golden brown, stirring regularly. Add the flour and cook for about a minute, stir in the white wine gradually and reduce by about half. Add the chicken stock and reduce by a further half. Whisk in the mustard, gherkins and finally the parsley.

Pour over the chops to serve.

Carmarthen Ham, Broad Beans, New Potatoes, Goat's Cheese Dressing

One of those dishes based on putting together a string of things that work well together. I kind of invented this myself. Except for the bits Maryann contributed and the ideas nicked from elsewhere. Well, nothing is really new, is it?

Carmarthen ham is an air-dried variety made by Albert Rees in Carmarthen market. If you can't get it then some form of Parma/Serrano/Bayonne will do. We use a goat's cheese from Talley in Carmarthenshire but others can be used (they must be soft, though).

You will need . . .

12 slices Carmarthen Ham
½ kilo young and small broad beans
½ kilo Pembrokeshire new potatoes
   (or substitute)
1 bunch spring onions, finely chopped
1 tbsp chopped chives

For the dressing...
100g soft goat's cheese
150ml white wine vinegar
100ml olive oil
Salt and pepper
2 tbsp white wine

Feeds four as a starter or serve for lunch with bread and maybe a green salad
or some dressed tomatoes with basil

Pod the broad beans and then blanche for one minute in lightly salted boiling water before plunging them into a bowl of iced water. Now remove the outer skin (this is a fine way to punish a small child). Clean the potatoes and cook until soft before cutting into bite-sized chunks. Crisp up four slices of the ham in a hot oven for about 5 minutes and tear the remaining ham into shreds. Crumble the goat's cheese into a bowl and, using a balloon whisk, gradually add the white wine vinegar until it forms a thin paste. Now add the oil slowly and whisk well until it thickens. If it gets too thick, add the wine to bring it back to a thinner consistency.

In a large bowl combine the potatoes, beans, shredded ham, spring onions and chives. Pour the dressing over and then divide onto four plates. Crumble the crispy ham onto the top of each serving.

Jambon Persillé (Jellied Ham with Parsley)

This is definitely in my top ten dishes of all time. I was first introduced to it about 20 years ago and I find it as appealing now as I did then. To me it's up there with the big hitters like a classic fish soup, coq au vin, côte de boeuf à la béarnaise, choucroute garnie. Dishes you would never want to say goodbye to or walk out on for a new model. I first had it cooked by my late mother-in-law, Jenny Willmott, who was an inspired cook. She'd make it in a glass bowl and turn it out as a perfect hemisphere of pink and green freshness. If I see it in a restaurant I usually order it and it's often what I choose at Y Polyn.

You will need . . .

2 smallish ham hocks, bone in and well rinsed
1 medium peeled onion
2 peeled carrots
1 leek
2 stalks celery

2 bay leaves
5 black peppercorns
4 gelatine leaves
4 tbsp parsley, finely chopped

Feeds loads

Put all the ingredients into a large stock pan and cover with water. Bring to the boil and skim off any scum from the surface. Turn down to a simmer and cook gently for at least 3 hours until the ham pull easily off the bone. Remove the hocks from the liquid and leave to cool until they can be comfortably handled. Strain the liquid through a sieve into a clean bowl. Measure ¾ litre of the liquor into a jug and leave to cool to blood temperature before adding the gelatine (you will need to have soaked this first according to the packet instructions) and stirring thoroughly. Shred the ham hocks into another bowl, discarding all bone and gristle, then stir in the parsley. Pack the meat and parsley mixture into a terrine of about 1½ litre capacity, pour the liquid over it and put in the fridge to set overnight. Slice and serve with your own piccalilli . . .

For the piccalilli you will need . . .

1 cauliflower	Mustard (Colmans)
½ cucumber	Sugar
1 red chilli	Cornflour
6 small shallots	1 tsp turmeric
Malt vinegar	1 tsp dill, finely chopped
White wine vinegar	150ml water
2 tsp salt	

Cut the cauliflower into florets. Peel the cucumber, deseed it and cut in half lengthways before slicing thinly. Deseed the chilli and chop very finely and cut the shallots into small chunks. Place the cauliflower, cucumber and shallots into a bowl, sprinkle with the salt and leave for around an hour. Put the sugar, mustard, turmeric and both vinegars into a saucepan and heat gently until dissolved before adding the chilli and simmering for 5 minutes. Blend the cornflour with the water and then whisk into the mustard mixture before simmering again for another 5 minutes.

Rinse the vegetables, drain well and add the chopped dill. Pour the hot mustard mixture over the vegetables and mix well until all are coated, then leave to cool. Pour into a sterilised jar or jars and place in the fridge. It's best to store for at least 10 days before using but it will last up to 6 months.

Middle White Pork Terrine

Of course, this doesn't have to be Middle White pork, but if it is, you can guarantee a special result with this dish. Most of the Middle White pigs in the UK seem to be owned by one man, Richard Vaughan. You might think this is greedy but I can only congratulate him on having the determination to stake his success on the special qualities of this rare breed pig. I have a few Middle Whites too, but not enough to share with anyone but the restaurant. So you can find Richard's pork (and beef) at www.huntsham.com.

You will need to start the night before . . .

½ kilo pork shoulder, cut into chunks

¼ kilo pork belly, cut into chunks

½ kilo pork liver, you guessed it

4 garlic cloves, thinly sliced

75ml brandy

Put the above together in a bowl and marinate overnight

100ml dry white wine

1 tbsp salt

½ tbsp ground black pepper

1 egg

10 rashers unsmoked back bacon

50ml cream

Feeds . . . this would make a robust starter for a dinner party of eight.
You wouldn't want to go too heavy on the main course, though.

Mince the marinated ingredients or, in the absence of a mincer, chop them up really finely. Whisk the egg, cream and seasoning together and then stir thoroughly into the meat mixture. Line a terrine (one with a capacity of about 1½ litres) with the strips of bacon and then pack in the meat mixture tightly before covering with the remaining bacon and a lid. Stand the terrine in a roasting tray, fill the tray half full with water and cover the whole thing with foil to create a *bain marie*. Bake in the oven at 170°C for 1¾ hours then remove the terrine and allow to cool. Ideally you'll want to put this in the fridge overnight and press by removing the lid and placing something heavy (like another terrine) on top.

Serve with gherkins or chutney and some good toast.

Crispy Pig's Ear Salad

Never underestimate the value of a pig's ear. It might not make a silk purse but it can be transformed into a number of delicious dishes including this little delight that Mark cooked for the pork episode of the programme.

You will need . . .

2 pig's ears
1 large onion
2 carrots
10 black peppercorns
A splash of vinegar

For the salad...
Seasonal salad leaves
2 shallots
A handful of capers

Put the non salad ingredients into a pan and add enough water to cover. Simmer the ears in the liquid for an hour. Remove the ears from the pan and slice thinly. Meanwhile prepare a salad using some seasonal leaves and adding thinly-sliced shallot and some capers. Dress the salad with some olive oil, a drizzle of fresh lemon juice and a grind of black pepper. Heat some more olive oil in a pan and when very hot toss in the strips of ear and let them fry until crisp and golden. Cast them onto the salad and serve to squeamish friends claiming it is crispy bacon before later revealing the truth.

Mark on pork

"My name is Mark and I'm a porkoholic. There; I've 'fessed up, the first of the twelve steps has been taken. My relationship with all things piggy has been obsessive for a long time and it seems likely to be a major contributor to my eventual cholesterol-choked demise.

What is it about pig meat that so attracts us? For me it's the versatility of the stuff that I love. You can do so much with a dead pig. Fergus Henderson, the chef-patron of London's St John restaurant, in the introduction to his classic cookbook *Nose to Tail Eating* states that 'There is a set of delights, textural and flavoursome, which lie beyond the fillet.' In those few short words he sets out a manifesto for an approach to cookery which has inspired a generation of chefs and restaurateurs. Many of today's most interesting restaurants are looking beyond the prime cuts of meat which for so long dominated menus. Loin of pork can be a delicious thing. Roasted, with crisp crackling and a moist tender interior, I can't think of a better centrepiece to Christmas lunch. That's far from the whole story with pork, however. For me it's the cheaper bits of pork that hold the most fascination.

Pigs' ears, poached for an hour then sizzled in a hot pan, make a delicious addition to an autumn salad. Pork belly cooked long and slow with oriental spices can be a succulent supper. The same belly, slow cooked and then crisped up in a hot oven and sliced thinly, can be the most delicious tapa.

Then there are trotters. Marco Pierre White made his name and his three Michelin stars serving a more refined version of Pierre Koffmann's pig's trotter, stuffed with morels and served with mash. I ate this dish when Marco was at his peak at The Restaurant in the Hyde Park Hotel. It was one of those deathbed dishes, one I will remember till that moment comes and one I will lament not eating again when I've joined the choir invisible.

I think I've made it clear that pork holds a very special place in both my heart and in my ample stomach but, as yet, I've not touched upon the ultimate expression of porcine delight. For me, ham is where it's at: French, Italian, Spanish and, indeed, Chris Rees's glorious Carmarthen Ham. I may lament the passing of Marco's trotters on my deathbed but I'll be doing so snacking on acorn-fed, Spanish, black-footed ham. **"**

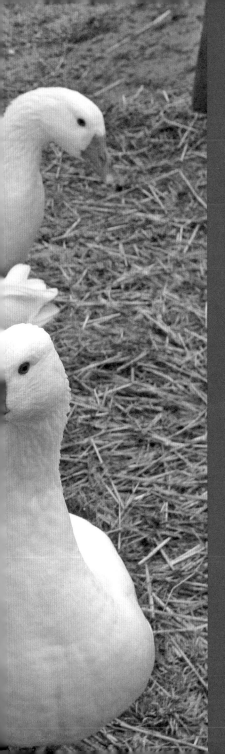

Goose
and some Duck

Let's face it, I've only been playing at farming.

Where I live I'm surrounded by agriculture and by people who make their living from it. I can't pretend that I've experienced anything but a tiny fraction of the pressures they face. It's a bit like the restaurant trade. Some of the people who come to eat with you must be pretty decent home cooks themselves, capable of serving up some really good food for their family and friends. But running a restaurant, serving meals to a packed dining room in a two-hour period, when you have no idea what they are going to order and everything is freshly prepared in your own kitchens – that's a whole other undertaking. At its peak, I had around 60 animals to attend to on my little piece of land and comparing that to real farming is much the same as comparing a dinner party for four to a Saturday night restaurant service for 50 people.

As an insight into the life of a farmer, mine was nothing more than a glimpse, a surreptitious peek through a crack in the door. But the little I saw was enough to open my eyes to at least some of the frustrations the agricultural community must suffer.

In a sense, it has been a small journey behind the headlines. In the last decade it seems to have been one food scare after another: BSE, foot and mouth, avian flu, blue tongue. During the year that we filmed there were outbreaks of both foot and mouth (courtesy of the Pirbright leakage) and avian flu. None of these incidents developed into the terrible epidemics that were threatened, yet both caused me some minor inconvenience and more than a small degree of concern. If I was troubled, how must the real farmer have been feeling?

*

I'd been to the poultry mart at Llandeilo once before, a research mission to find out what was available when the time came to acquire the stock. It was geese I was especially interested in. The chickens I already had and I was planning to get ducks from the same supplier, but the mart was the place to get the geese. There was no shortage on offer at that first visit. The undercover auction was a seething mass of bird life, row after row of caged poultry of all descriptions, from the beautiful to the bizarre: birds for showing, birds for laying and birds for eventual eating. I checked out the goslings, young, fluffy and available in some abundance. I'd return a month later, to the next scheduled market and buy the stock I needed. The timing was good; by then I'd have their home ready, the pond dug out, lined and filled.

I had something different in mind when it came to eating the geese. I wanted to serve them up at some kind of celebratory meal at Y Polyn, an occasion to thank the people who had helped me along the way. It would be

held just before Christmas and the schedule looked good; there would be just enough fattening time to ensure the birds would be ready in time.

Four weeks on, I arrived at the market with my wife and my youngest son. The camera crew had arranged to be there before us and had set up in the huge shed that had been such a festival of feathers, beaks and claws just a month before. As I approached the entrance I began to feel something wasn't right; where there should have been noise there was silence. Inside, as before, I saw row upon row of cages – but today we were the only people in there and the metal-barred boxes, they were all empty! In these situations my instinct is to panic and wonder how I managed to mess up this time. I must have got the date wrong – but that couldn't be; I'd called to check only two days before and I'd even made sure that there would be some goslings there. The time: were we too late? I checked the programme and saw that, if anything, we were early. The camera crew just followed me around capturing my bemusement and confusion. Their presence was part of the problem – had I dragged them down here for no reason? Filming isn't cheap and our available days were limited; if I'd wasted one I was going to be less than popular with the production company.

Outside, the rest of the mart was as busy as ever. In tandem with the poultry sale they always held an auction of farm machinery and equipment and the pitches were crowded with prospective buyers. There I spotted a man with a clipboard, a sure sign of authority. What had happened to the poultry mart?

Bird flu, in north Wales, a small outbreak but enough to necessitate the closure of all poultry markets in Wales. 'There'll be one in a month,' the man told me, 'assuming there are no more outbreaks.' A month would be too late for me; I hadn't bargained on any kind of delay. We got back in the car and headed off towards home. As it happened, the Pontargothi Show, the first agricultural show of the season and our local event, was taking place the same day. Surely somebody there would know where I could get some goslings in a hurry.

I headed for the beer tent. Much of the help I'd had in this whole farming enterprise had come from my friend Steve Smythe, so finding him seemed a good next move. My guess was he'd be into his second or third pint by now – an educated guess, based on the fact that if I hadn't been filming I'd have been with him. As it turned out, I was right about his whereabouts, though slightly out on the number of pints. I went to the bar and bought him another (and one for me, so he wouldn't feel awkward).

'Steve, I need to get some goslings urgently. Do you know anyone who keeps goslings?'

'No.'

'What do you mean "no"? You're a farmer; you must know *someone* who keeps them.'

Steve gave me that exasperated look that I'd seen many times before. The look that said 'You are so bloody naïve, is it really worth me wasting my breath?' Only it was better this time because he had clearly had more than several beers and my questions were forcing him to try and concentrate and that was a real burden. He looked confused and I waited while he gathered his thoughts.

'You see, the thing is,' he eventually began, and then paused. 'The thing is, that ducks are what farmers' wives used to keep for Christmas. But they don't do it anymore.'

He shook his head in certainty and stopped talking, obviously relieved, even triumphant, to have dealt with the query and be free now to move on to less taxing matters. I, on the other hand, was just beginning to enjoy the encounter – sometimes it can be entertaining to be totally sober in the presence of those less so. It's a novelty.

'But Steve, I'm not looking for ducks, I'm after goslings.'

Steve looked at me quizzically. I think that by this point he may well have forgotten the original question.

'Goslings too,' he said with finality.

To be fair, Steve's not a poultry man; he keeps sheep and cattle and quite a few children too. I left him to his beer, hoping I could join him later, if he was still standing.

Wandering around the show I saw plenty of animals but none of them were birds – unsurprising really, given that the show was under the same restrictions as the mart people in Llandeilo. Nevertheless, the fields were filled with farming folk; it's an important agricultural show, thousands attend and it stood to reason that somebody must keep geese. I asked a few people, randomly and to no effect, before my desperation drove me to the announcers' hut where I put out a plea across the whole showground. That was bound to work.

Sure enough, after a few minutes a chap arrived at the hut.

'I've got a dozen or so goslings available,' he said. This was sounding encouraging.

'You have? What are they?'

'Grey geese, Canada Grey.'

"Oh? How do they taste?'

'Bloody awful.'

And that was it, until I got a call from a friend in St Davids, Pembrokeshire, who'd managed to locate half a dozen Embden geese, the breed I'd been looking for. So I shot down there and picked them up.

*

In many ways the geese were simple to look after and they matured without a hitch. I'd been warned that they'd grow to quite a size and was further cautioned that they might be aggressive at times. It's true that as they reached adulthood they became increasingly independent in their outlook. They had a swagger about them that said they weren't about to be messed with, and much of their energy seemed to be devoted to warding off threats that weren't really there. Their paddock was sandwiched between those occupied by the pigs and the chickens, and the shared borders seemed to be a constant source of concern for them. Maybe it was the fact that they were surrounded that induced some kind of paranoia. Personally I somehow doubt that the pigs and the chickens had formed a strategic alliance or that both were effectively the stooges of the mighty Welsh Black cattle located in a more distant field – nevertheless, the situation had an air of Russia and the Caucases about it. Each morning I'd open the door of the goose shed and they'd burst out, their emergence accompanied by the piercing, machine-gun staccato of their honking. They'd immediately make for the fence that separated them from the pigs and deliver a volley of aggressive, neck-out abuse at the porkers, who would be quietly eating their food. Bellicose language wouldn't be enough, though; if they could reach, the geese would steal the pigs' food and if that failed, they would nip the pigs instead, tails and ears being the favoured targets. The pigs dealt with all this by simply ignoring the geese, presumably in the belief that they'd get bored soon enough and go away. It was a clever tactic. The geese rarely persisted long once they realised the pigs weren't rising to the bait so they'd charge across to the other fence and intimidate the chickens instead. I have to say they never attempted to bite me. We had our disagreements, chiefly at bed time when it could take 20 minutes to round them up if they were feeling especially stubborn.

But it was all sound and fury, signifying not very much. When the geese went I missed them. I missed them in the way that you miss a houseful of warring kids. You can't wait to be rid of them but once they're gone, you'd kill to have that cacophony back.

And the ducks? They were picture-book specimens until someone upset them . . .

As is my nature, I'd like to end on a note of failure – I feel more comfortable that way. The geese were meant to share their space with some ducks. I'd built a pond so that the two species could splash about a bit together and do all that waterfowl stuff – glide, preen, shake their feathers dry.

The ducks were a disaster. I started off with a dozen ducklings, a couple of days old and unfeasibly cute. They were a mass of fluffy yellow, with bright, round eyes and pale pink bills. They had the same need for incubation as the chicks and needed careful temperature control too. The first day or two went by without incident but then one of the ducks appeared to have some kind of cold, breathing heavily and listless, with little enthusiasm for eating. I tried feeding it through a syringe but it showed no interest; its decline was irreversible, it seemed, and it died within 24 hours. And then another one followed it. The next morning I opened their shed to see two more ducklings lying on their backs, webbed feet in the air, motionless. I rang Steve Merritt, my poultry-farming friend who had got the birds for me, and found he'd been trying to get in touch with me as well. The fowl had turned out to be a bad batch, hatched into some mouldy bedding and susceptible to pneumonia. Quite a few of his ducklings had perished too.

In the end only four survived. Maybe it was survival of the fittest because these four birds were certainly fighters. They fought each other, constantly. One was such a bully that I eventually had to separate him out because he was biting lumps out of the others' wings. When I eventually returned him to his peers they had gathered enough courage to take their revenge and then it was his turn to be lacerated by the others. It seemed that once they had the taste for blood there was no going back. I learned a lot of things from this farming lark and one thing I know for certain: you can't reason with a psychopathic duck.

Goose Rillettes

A rillette is basically a paté-style dish made by slow-cooking heavily salted meat in fat until it can be easily shredded and then potted before being served cold with toast. You may have noticed the use of all the key words there: meat, slow cooking, salt, fat — is it any wonder they are so delicious? At Y Polyn we make pork and duck examples, too, (you can use the same recipe for the latter, allowing 6 legs) but the goose one is especially rich and gamey.

You will need . . .

4 goose legs

4 garlic cloves

2 sprigs of thyme

1tsp cumin and fennel seeds

Salt and pepper

500ml white wine

Feeds about 8 as a starter or snack.

Place the goose legs in a roasting tray, season them well and sprinkle over the cumin and fennel seeds. Roast at 180°C for 45 minutes to 1 hour until cooked and golden brown. Transfer to a large saucepan with all the juices, add the garlic and herbs and then the wine. Bring the saucepan up to a very gentle simmer then cover and cook for 1½ hours when the meat should be falling off the bone.

Remove from the heat and cool until comfortable to handle then tear off the skin and discard. Next, loosen the flesh from all the bones and shred roughly into a clean bowl. Add all the juices from the casserole dish and mix well. If a little dry, you can add some extra melted goose fat; you are looking for a very moist consistency.

Pack the goose into ramekins so that you have about 8 portions. Place in the fridge to set for at least 24 hours. You should remove them from the fridge half an hour before serving otherwise they will be too cold, with a consequent loss of flavour. All you need now is some hot toast and a sharp chutney to cut through the fat.

Duck Confit, Braised Lentils and Pancetta

When I inspected restaurants for a living it was routine to find duck confit on menus. Mostly they were pretty awful examples, leathery on the outside and dried out within. What you want, of course, is a crispy skin shrouding rich, moist meat. Confit has become a much misused term, particularly by adolescent chefs seeking to pimp up their menu descriptions. The word comes from the French for 'preserve', so it only makes sense where foods have been immersed in a substance for preservation (and taste). One example is fruit preserved in sugar, another is meat preserved in its own fat, which is where this dish made its entrance.

You will need to start the day before . . .
- 4 duck legs
- 2 garlic cloves
- 2 sprigs of thyme
- Pepper and sea salt
- 1 litre duck fat

Crush the garlic and mix with the thyme leaves and season with a good grind of pepper and a liberal sprinkling of sea salt. Blend this well and then rub it into the duck legs. Cover this and leave to marinate overnight. The next day place the duck legs into a roasting tray – they need to be snug, so take care with the size. Melt the duck fat and pour it over the legs to cover. Cover this with baking parchment and then foil and place in an oven at 130°C for 3 hours until the duck legs feel cooked and tender. Remove from the roasting tray and place in a clean container, pour the duck fat from the tray over them and leave to cool before placing in the fridge. The duck legs will keep like this (as long as covered in fat) for a good month.

To reheat, dig the legs out and ensure they are free of the fat. Melt a tablespoon of the fat in a heavy frying pan and when hot add the duck legs skin side down, cook for 3 or 4 minutes until starting to colour, turn over and place in a hot oven at 200°C for about 15 minutes until crispy and golden brown. Serve with the lentils . . .

You will need for the lentils . . .

- 100g lentils du Puy (small French green lentils)
- 50g pancetta
- 1 carrot
- 1 celery stalk
- 1 tbsp olive oil
- 2 shallots
- 1 bunch chives, finely chopped
- 100ml chicken stock (see page 138)

Soak the lentils overnight in water, then drain and rinse. Place the lentils in cold water, bring to the boil and then simmer gently for 20 minutes. Chop the pancetta into small dice, sizzle in olive oil in a large frying pan until cooked and starting to brown. Peel and chop the carrot, shallots and celery into small dice of the same size as the pancetta. Add these to the pancetta in the pan and cook for a couple of minutes, until starting to soften. Drain the lentils and put in a clean saucepan, add the pancetta and the vegetables and the chicken stock, season and simmer for 5 to 10 minutes until the lentils are tender. You should be left with moist lentils in a very light amount of broth – you may need to add a little more stock to achieve this.

Roast Goose

This is what I made in the final episode of 'The Wright Taste', assisted by Stephen Jones, Dwayne Peel and Bruce Douglas. The softly spoken Scotland prop was a real bonus, because he wants to run his own restaurant when he quits rugby and he knows his way around a kitchen. Stephen and Dwayne were typically enthusiastic and, for my part, I was pleased not to descend into blind panic. I've always cooked but I'm not cut out to run a restaurant kitchen; the multi-tasking doesn't agree with me. We got the food out but the goose was well and truly (over) cooked. I checked a number of recipes which varied wildly before deciding on a cooking time and eventually went with something in the middle. My experiences suggest that the cooking time for a typical 6-kilo goose is as little as one hour and 30 minutes. Fast and hot is the method.

You will need . . .

6 kilo goose

3 lemons

Black pepper and sea salt

They say a goose this size feeds as many as ten, but I think that's pushing it a bit.
I'd say a maximum of eight. Six would have a feast.

Trim any excess fat from the goose and remove the giblets, then prick the skin all over. Zest the lemons and then cut them into halves. Mix a handful of sea salt with the zest and a few grinds of pepper and rub the mix into the skin of the goose. Push the halved lemons into the neck end of the bird. Preheat the oven to 250°C and place the goose on a rack in a roasting tray breast side up. After 15 minutes turn the oven down to 180°C, then, after an hour, remove the goose and cut around the thighs to open up the legs a little – this helps to make sure that whole bird cooks at the same pace. You might want to pour some fat out of the pan at this point (it's ideal, of course, for roasting potatoes). Return the bird for the last half-hour of cooking. You can check the internal temperature with a probe to the thickest part of the thigh – it will need to reach 70°C.

For the gravy you can use the chicken stock on page 138, or make a stock using the same method but using the giblets instead of the chicken bones. When the goose is cooked, take it off the pan and leave to rest for 20 minutes. Put the roasting tray over heat, sprinkle in a dessertspoon of cornflower and gradually add 250ml of cider, scraping all the tasty brown bits from the pan. Let this bubble away whilst gradually adding 250ml of the stock. Bring to the boil and then strain through a sieve into a saucepan before reducing by about half. Whisk in a couple of small knobs of butter at the last minute to add a little shine to the sauce.

You can serve this with mash and braised red cabbage, or you may prefer roast potatoes cooked in the goose fat.

Roast Boned and Stuffed Barbary Duck, Sweet Red Wine Sauce

In their live state, Barbary ducks are more commonly known as Muscovy. With their carbuncles and clawed feet they're not about to win any beauty pageants for waterfowl and as I learned, they can have anger management issues too. They taste great, though, and this is another recipe based on something my mother-in-law Jenny used to make. If boning the thing out is a bit of a challenge, either find a butcher who will do it or buy them ready prepared.

You will need . . .

1 whole Barbary duck, boned out

1 onion, finely chopped

2 cloves garlic, finely chopped

50g pancetta, finely chopped

1 tbsp parsley as above

100g white breadcrumbs

25g dried apricots

25g dried prunes

25g butter

Salt and pepper

1tbsp clear honey

250ml fruity red wine (an Oz shiraz for example)

250ml chicken stock

Feeds two . . . you'll need half a duck per person.

Melt the butter in a frying pan and fry the pancetta to render the fat out of it and then add the onion and garlic, cooking until softened. Add these to the breadcrumbs in a large bowl with the parsley and fold gently together.

Lay the duck on its back and place the stuffing in a long sausage along its length. Lay the fruit along the stuffing and then roll the duck meat around the mixture so you have an oval cylinder. Sew up neatly with some string, using a cook's needle and ensuring the stuffing is completely sealed in, then turn the bird over and prick the skin in its entirety with a sharp skewer or needle. Season the skin well with salt and pepper.

Put in a roasting tin and roast for 45 minutes at 200°C. Remove from the oven and drizzle with the honey and return to the oven for another 15 minutes before removing and leaving to rest on a board for 20 minutes. Spoon off the excess fat in the pan leaving the roasting juices in the tin. Add to them the red wine and, over a medium heat, scrape up all the duck and honey residues. Simmer for 5 minutes, then add the chicken stock and simmer for a further 5 minutes. Strain this liquor into a clean saucepan and reduce by simmering until you have a dark and slightly sticky sauce.

Carve the duck into about 8 thick slices and drizzle with the sauce.

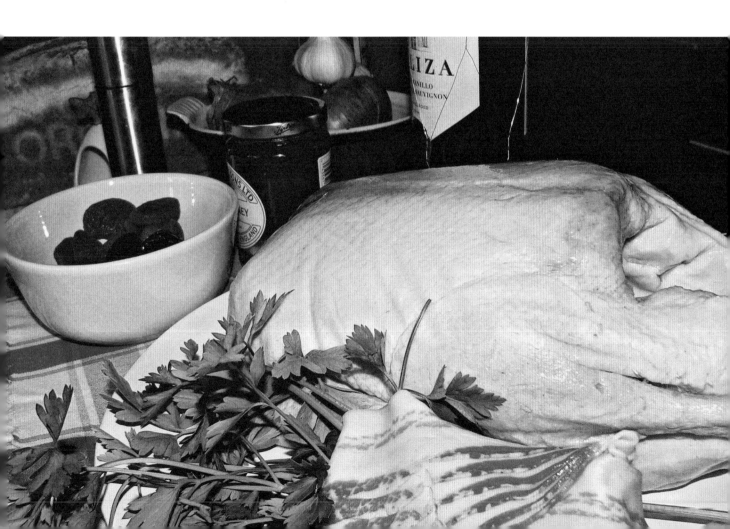

Mark on goose

"This is not the place to get into a debate on the rights and wrongs of eating foie gras but, in truth, I've eaten more of this particular treat than I've ever eaten goose meat itself. If a restaurant has ambitions to be seen as 'exclusive' or 'up-market' there's a fair chance that the stuff will turn up on a menu from time to time. We have served it at Y Polyn but, I think, only once. Perhaps this says more about how we want the restaurant to be viewed, inclusive rather than exclusive, than it does about our own feelings regarding the rights and wrongs of the stuff.

What little goose I have eaten tended to be served in places which have a German or Austrian behind the stoves. The hugely under-rated chef Gerald Röser who had a great little restaurant on Hastings sea front and is now cooking at the Grand Hotel in Eastbourne used to serve a fantastic Goose breast dish with cabbage, bacon and juniper berries. I also seem to recall the great Austrian chef Peter Hauser serving goose at his sweet little country house hotel Stock Hill at Gillingham. Perhaps our Germanic cousins appreciate that goose somehow sits between those more delicate birds like chicken and guinea fowl and more robust game birds like grouse and pheasant.

Goose really comes into its own when it is the centrepiece of a big family meal like Christmas lunch. Perhaps because as it cooks it gives of the most delicious fat I can think of for roasting spuds. We bought a most magnificent organically reared goose from our great friends Steve and Juliet at S&J organics in Carmarthenshire this year and the goose ably assisted by a loin of Simon's middle white was the focus for perhaps the tastiest Christmas lunch I have ever demolished.

I recently found out that what is now the car park at the restaurant used to be the staging area for walking the local farm produced geese to market in time for Christmas. It sounds quite barbaric but the poor birds would have their feet tarred to protect them on the march towards their festive doom. Perhaps we should have more of the stuff on the menu to commemorate the Christmas muster in years gone by. "

Other Stuff

You may have noticed that this book has been cleverly structured to fit in with the episode structure of *The Wright Taste.* That leaves us without any puds, of course. Well, I guess we can live with that for now; after all, this is a book about producing and eating meat. It seemed churlish though not to give you some clues on how we make some of the dishes that we suggest as accompaniments to the meat recipes. We've also thrown in a couple of bread recipes because that's fundamental to what we offer at Y Polyn and it's hard to have a good meal without good bread, isn't it?

Mark's Sourdough

Mark makes this at Y Polyn. Naturally, he followed some well-worn recipes but it's one of those things where you have to develop a feel for what you are doing. I can testify to the fact that he's done that because this bread has simply got better as time has gone on. Jay Rayner compared it to the legendary Poilane in his 'Observer' column — praise indeed. This is Mark's recipe, so these are his words.

You will need . . .

1.5 litres sourdough starter
1 litre tepid water
1 kilo T55 baguette flour

1 kilo unbleached organic stoneground flour (we use flour from Bacheldre Mill in Montgomeryshire)
7tsp fine ground sea salt
Semolina for dusting

Makes six loaves

Baking differs from regular cooking in that accuracy in weighing ingredients is quite important but there is a bit of leeway with proportions. The weather is a factor as can be the particular batch of flour you use. Hot weather makes bread rise more quickly and some flours can be more hydrated than others, even those from the same mill.

I'm assuming that you will have access to a batch of active sourdough starter which, I admit, is a big assumption. You can find lots of recipes for creating a starter on the net or, if you find yourself in west Wales, do drop in and I'll be happy to give you some of our homegrown starter. Our starter has been alive for just over two years and, provided you remember to feed it, it's pretty tolerant of occasional neglect.

I bake solely by hand because I love the feeling of actually working the dough rather than relying on a food mixer to develop the all important gluten network. The recipe takes a while to complete. I start it off at about 9am and the loaves are ready to go into the oven at 6pm, but the individual steps are both simple and short. It's the waiting for stuff to happen that takes up all that time.

Weigh out the starter into a big bowl and whisk in the tepid water. Weigh the two flours and salt and add all three to the water and starter mix. Then it's time to get your hands in and to bring together the mixture till it forms a soft dough. Cover with a wet tea towel and leave for about an hour in a warm place until the flour has become thoroughly hydrated. Now it's time for the first kneading. You don't need to spend ages on this. 30 seconds to a minute's worth of stretching and folding is quite sufficient. You should see at this stage that the dough becomes smoother and much more elastic. Cover the bowl with your wet tea towel and tuck it back in its cosy corner for another hour to relax and start fermenting.

When you came back this time you should see that the dough has increased in volume and is beginning to develop some bubbles of gas. Knead the dough for another minute or so and tuck the covered bowl back in its warm place for another hour or so. One more round of kneading and resting and you will be ready to shape your loaves. Divide your dough into six equal portions and give each a final kneading, shaping each piece firstly into a tight ball and then into a neat rugby ball shape. Sourdough is much wetter than yeast-leavened bread dough and it needs some support to hold its shape while it proves. I prove the bread in those oval woven breadbaskets lined with napkins, which are liberally sprinkled with semolina. Leave the shaped loaves to prove in their baskets for 3-4 hours depending on the ambient temperature. Once the loaves have doubled in size turn them out on to an oiled and semolina-dusted baking sheet. Slash the tops 4-5 times and bake in a hot oven 200°C for about 45 mins, until the crust has developed and the loaves sound hollow when tapped.

Focaccia

If it's good, it's light, oily and crisp on top. Sometimes they use other toppings at Y Polyn like feta and tomato or black olives. Personally I disagree with this because it reminds me of pizza and that seems inappropriate as an accompaniment to a meal. But then, I'm a man of simple tastes . . .

You will need . . .

- 1 tbsp caster sugar
- 1 heaped tbsp dried yeast
- ½ pint cold milk
- ½ pint boiling water
- 2lb strong white bread flour

- 1 tbsp salt
- 2 tbsp olive oil
- 1 egg
- Rosemary
- Sea salt

Feeds around 12

Combine milk, boiling water, sugar and then sprinkle in the yeast. Leave this until it bubbles. Add the flour, 1 tablespoon of the olive oil, the egg and the salt and mix well. Leave in a warm place to prove until doubled in size (about an hour). Knock down and knead well into a ball then roll out into a rectangular shape about an inch thick. Place this on an oiled baking tray. Leave in a warm place again until risen double, with the surface slightly bubbly. Now sprinkle the rosemary and sea salt on top of the bread randomly and poke into the dough with your fingers so it resembles a buttoned mattress. Leave to rest for five minutes and then bake at 200°C for 25 minutes. Remove and drizzle with olive oil whilst still warm on a rack.

Braised Red Cabbage with Apples

We made this to go with the roast goose. I think Stephen Jones and Dwayne Peel both had a hand in it and the result was pretty good. Later Dwayne rang and asked to be reminded of the recipe so he could cook it for his family's Christmas lunch. I forgot to ask him how it went.

You will need . . .

1 red cabbage, washed and shredded

1 Bramley apple, peeled, cored and sliced

1 onion, finely chopped

500ml dry cider

Salt and pepper

100g butter

Melt the butter in a large heavy saucepan. Add the onion and apple and cook until the onion softens. Now add the red cabbage and stir until it is coated in the butter. Add the cider, bring to the boil and then turn down to a gentle simmer. Season this and then cook for around 2½ hours, stirring every 20 minutes or so to prevent the cabbage catching on the bottom of the pan. The cabbage should be glossy and tender.

Green Cabbage, Leek and Spinach

I could eat this on its own, but rarely do.

You will need . . .

1 primo or pointed cabbage

4 leeks, cleaned

250g baby spinach

100g butter

Salt and pepper

Cut the leek into 1cm rounds and cut the cabbage into quarters (after removing the outer leaves). Melt the butter in a saucepan over a medium heat and cook the leeks in the butter for about five minutes, stirring all the time. Next add the cabbage and cook for another minute or two before adding the spinach for the final few seconds. The cabbage should still be crispy when served.

Creamy Garlic Potatoes

Sort of dauphinoise, but delicious by any name.

You will need . . .

1kilo Maris Piper potatoes, peeled

6 garlic cloves thinly sliced

Salt and pepper

200ml double cream

50g white breadcrumbs mixed with finely

chopped parsley

Slice the potatoes thinly (about the thickness of a 50p coin) and layer these in a buttered baking dish with the garlic and plenty of seasoning – three layers should do it. Season the top layer and then pour over the cream until it is about ⅔ of the way to the top. Cover with baking parchment and foil and bake at 190°C for around an hour until well cooked. These are ready immediately but are just as good reheated. To serve or to reheat, spoon them into a serving dish, sprinkle with the breadcrumb mix and crisp up in a hot oven for 20 minutes.

Mash

The more butter the better in my opinion. Use potatoes that are best for mashing like Cara, Desirée or Estima. You can add stuff like garlic or spring onion and chive if you want to vary it a bit.

You will need . . .

1 kilo potatoes peeled

1 tbsp salt

200g melted butter

Cut the potatoes into even sized pieces and cover with cold water and add the salt. Bring this up to the boil and cook for around 15 minutes until tender. Mash whilst still hot, adding the butter and stir thoroughly.

To make garlic mash, put 10 peeled garlic cloves with 100ml of cream in a saucepan, bring to the boil and then simmer for 20 minutes. Blend using a stick blender and add to the potatoes. For spring onion and chive, simply chop them finely and stir into the mash.

Braised Fennel in Cider

We often serve this at Y Polyn and it has its fans.

You will need . . .

6 bulbs of fennel
100g of butter

Salt and pepper
1 litre dry cider

Trim the fennel at the top and the bottom, removing the outer layer if it looks coarse or discoloured. Cut it into quarters and place in a single layer in a roasting tray. Season this well and dot with small cubes of the butter then pour in the cider and cover with baking parchment and foil to allow the fennel to steam in the tray. Cook for around an hour until very tender at about 170°C.

Chicken Stock

I know you've heard it all before but so much good food starts with a decent stock. Some of the stuff you can buy now isn't too bad, especially the liquid bouillons. Marco Pierre White swears by a Knorr stock cube apparently. You may wish to take him seriously.

You will need . . .

Raw carcass of two chickens, roughly chopped
1 carrot, peeled
2 sticks celery
1 onion, peeled and halved

6 bay leaves
Sprig parsley
6 black peppercorns
1 leek, trimmed and cleaned

Put the chicken bit in the roasting tray and roast in a hot oven at 200°C for 30 minutes. Place in a large casserole dish with the vegetables, herbs and the peppercorns. Cover with cold water and bring to the boil before simmering for at least 6 hours – all day is better (Skim the surface periodically). Cool and strain through a fine sieve. This will keep for five days in the fridge.

Epilogue

It seems a little pathetic now but I'll admit to you there were times when I was scared. It was the fear of the unknown really, the first animals arriving on the land, the challenge of keeping day-old chicks alive, the trips to the abattoir. Everything was new to me and I probably learned more than I now realise. Of course, it was rewarding – there's something especially nourishing about eating meat from animals that you raised yourself and it's even more satisfying to serve it to other people and have them sing its praises. I loved the discipline of it, too. Of having to get up earlier than I would normally contemplate, feed a load of animals before I even thought about feeding myself. The majesty of the sunrise in the Tywi valley is the kind of splendour you know is worth getting out of bed for but you rarely do. I had to, and I was grateful for that.

When the filming ended, the farming didn't. As I write, I still have pigs and sheep, including our own lambs. And as time goes on I think we'll be looking to expand the amount of meat we produce ourselves, not least because we have another restaurant project planned for North Dock in Llanelli with our partners Stephen Jones, Dwayne Peel and Robert Williams.

Along the way I met some inspiring people involved in farming and food in Wales. For me, that is no surprise. I've long been aware of the riches that my home country has to offer in terms of great things to eat. As someone who made a career of eating out across the UK, I guess I'm pretty well-placed to assess where we stand as a country in terms of our food culture. One thing is obvious: there have been huge steps forward. There are many better places to eat; the quality and marketing of the food we produce has increased exponentially, and the public interest in food and its origin is on a whole different level to where it was a couple of decades ago. But let's not forget, you could say all those things about the rest of the UK – and if I'm completely honest, I'm disappointed that we're not more ambitious about our food culture in Wales. With an economy heavily reliant upon agriculture and tourism, the importance of our food offering should be apparent to anyone.

And it's true this hasn't gone unnoticed and there have been a myriad of initiatives over recent years, emanating from quangos like the WDA and the Welsh

Tourist Board and more recently from the Welsh Assembly Government that eventually gobbled them up. Some have been effective, others less so. One thing's for sure: a lot of money has been spent. In my view, for what it's worth, we're still suffering from a lack of nerve. The opportunity exists to really make a name for ourselves as a food nation and steal a march on our neighbours and the way to do that is through education. Others are talking about it, true, but while they're talking we in Wales should get on with it.

To me, it's a disgrace that children leave education without the ability to cook, with no understanding of food and its origin and with little respect for its importance. Few things are more fundamental to our existence. We eat every day, repeatedly; food dominates our shopping habits; it takes a good chunk of most people's disposable income – and yet generations leave our schools in complete culinary ignorance. We hear so much about healthy eating but if we're really going to change attitudes then we need to allow our children to learn how to cook and to take pleasure in cooking. In our restaurants, too, those who aspire to quality are crying out for young chefs who have a real understanding of food and a genuine love of cooking. If those people were available it would revolutionise the quality of our restaurant offerings. I don't think any of this is impossible.

Is it really too ambitious to imagine a training kitchen in every secondary school in Wales and a curriculum that ensures that all students get a basic grounding in the subject, with those who show real enthusiasm having the opportunity to develop further? Some would say it's unrealistic to jam more into an already crowded schedule. I think the opposite is true: we can't afford not to take this opportunity to be a nation that actually converts all the fine words about food culture into practice, leaving others in our culinary wake. What it needs is ambition, determination and vision – don't laugh: maybe somebody will surprise us.

Acknowledgements

Two people I need to thank above all others: Maryann, without whom little is possible, and my friend Steve Smythe, a man loved by all (with good reason).

The risk of a list like this is that you leave someone out. I'm sure I will have done so, and apologise in advance for any omissions. They will be down to memory rather than lack of appreciation.

Anyway, my thanks go to:

Arwyn Allen, Marian Allen, Alix Alliston, Heston Blumenthal, Pip Broughton, Julian Castaldi, Anthony Davies, Wyn Davies, Barry Davies, Ivor Davies, Bruce Douglas, Aled Eirug, Chris Galvin, Jeff Galvin, Maryann Gilchrist, The Hepburns, Shaun Hill, Andrew James, Anthony James, John James, Les James, Mairwen Jones, Stephen Jones, Wyn Jones, Glyn Lenton, Huw Lloyd, Mark Manson, Susan Manson, Ellie McNair, Steve Merrit, Jamie Owen, Dwayne Peel, John Pratt, Gordon Ramsay, Sian Rees, Maggie Russell, Steve Smith, Amy Tanner, Stephen Terry, Catrin Thomas, Dorian Thomas, Robert Williams, Bill Willmott, Amanda Windsor, Anita Wright, Tony Wright, Joel Wright and many others.

Additional photographs are included by permission of The Welsh Black Cattle Society (pp. 64, 66) and Jamie Wright (pp. 8, 40, 61, 101, 109, 127).

Recipe Index